The
CYNIC'S GUIDE
to Coping with Life

The
CYNIC'S GUIDE
to Coping with Life

Edited by
Pamela Chichinskas and Lynette Stokes
with contributions from
Nicholas Pashley Anthony Jenkins Larry Tyson

Eden Press
Montréal

THE CYNIC'S GUIDE TO COPING WITH LIFE
Edited by Pamela Chichinskas and Lynette Stokes

ISBN: 0-920792-90-1

Cover design: EDDESIGN
Cover illustration: Larry Tyson
Inside page design: Pamela Chichinskas and Lynette Stokes

Printed in Canada at Metropole Litho Inc.
Dépot légel — quatrième trimestre 1987
Bibliothèque nationale du Québec

Eden Press
31A Westminster Avenue
Montreal, Quebec
H4X 1Y8

Canadian Cataloguing in Publication Data

Chichinskas, Pamela
    The cynic's guide to coping with life

ISBN 0-920792-90-1

    1. Cynicism--Anecdotes, facetiae, satire, etc.
I. Stokes, Lynette.   II. Title.

PN6178.C3C44 1987   828'.0208   C87-090233-4

To cynics everywhere

TABLE OF CONTENTS

INTRODUCTION 13

WHAT'S POLLYANNA DONE LATELY?
Being a Cynic in the 1980s
      Nicholas Pashley 15

HOW TO COPE WITH BEING ELVIS PRESLEY'S LOVE CHILD
      Nicholas Pashley 17

WHAT DID THE PRESIDENT FORGET
And When Did He Forget It?
      Nicholas Pashley 21

PRESIDENT REAGAN CARTOON
      Larry Tyson 23

MOTHER GROUSE
      Larry Tyson 25

COPING WITH CULTURE
How To Enjoy A Night At The Opera
Even If The Marx Brothers Aren't In It
      Nicholas Pashley 29

COPING WITH SNOBS
      Anthony Jenkins 34

COPING WITH LOVE GODDESSES OF THE EIGHTIES
Bad Girls of Our Time
      Nicholas Pashley 37

THE TEN COMMANDMENTS OF THE TRENDY
      Anthony Jenkins 41

THE HORSEMEN OF THE PETTY ANNOYANCE
      Anthony Jenkins 42

A LISTENERS' GUIDE TO CONTEMPORARY RADIO
      Nicholas Pashley 44

YOU KNOW IT'S GOING TO BE 'ONE OF THOSE DAYS' WHEN:
Anthony Jenkins...46

IT'S IN THE STARS
Coping With the New Astrology
Nicholas Pashley
Illustrated by Larry Tyson.............................47

COPING WITH INTROSPECTION
Lynette Stokes..54

GREAT MOMENTS IN THE HISTORY OF NON-SMOKING
Anthony Jenkins.......................................58

COPING WITH MEN
A Beginner's Guide for Women
Nicholas Pashley......................................62

CARTOON
Larry Tyson...63

COPING WITH THE OPPOSITE SEX
Things to Avoid in a Mate
Anthony Jenkins.......................................67

COPING WITH WOMEN
A Beginner's Guide for Men
Nicholas Pashley......................................69

CARTOON
Larry Tyson...70

CARTOON
Larry Tyson...73

COPING WITH THE OPPOSITE SEX
'Personals' Columns Explained
Anthony Jenkins.......................................74

COPING WITH GOD
Nicholas Pashley......................................76

SEVEN MORE DEADLY SINS
Anthony Jenkins.......................................81

TEN REASONS TO STAY ALIVE
The Cynic's Guide To The Future
Nicholas Pashley.......................................82

COPING WITH ADVERSITY
If It Wasn't For Bad Luck
I Wouldn't Have No Luck At All
Nicholas Pashley.......................................85

COPING WITH SOCIETY'S PROBLEMS
Knowing Where to Place the Blame
Anthony Jenkins.......................................88

SNIDES
Larry Tyson.......................................89

HOW TO MAKE FRIENDS AND USE PEOPLE
Pamela Chichinskas.......................................92

HOW CELEBRITIES COPE
Anthony Jenkins.......................................95

DR. RUT RULES FOR COPING WITH MODERN SEXUALITY
Anthony Jenkins.......................................96

COPING WITH TRAVEL
Nicholas Pashley.......................................98

COPING WITH DEJA VU
Why The Eighties Are Like The Fifties
Nicholas Pashley.......................................103

COPING WITH THE RICH
Anthony Jenkins.......................................105

NReh?
Anthony Jenkins.......................................106

COPING WITH POPULAR MUSIC
Separating Myth From Reality
Nicholas Pashley.......................................108

COPING WITH THE FUTURE
Anthony Jenkins... 111

COPING WITH GETTING OLDER
Nicholas Pashley.. 113

COPING WITH THE LANGUAGE OF BUSINESS
Anthony Jenkins... 116

THE TROUBLE WITH SPORTS
Take Me Out of the Ballgame
Nicholas Pashley.. 118

EMILY PILLAR'S ETIQUETTE FOR THE EIGHTIES
Anthony Jenkins... 122

CARTOON
Larry Tyson... 124

WHY WORK FOR A LIVING
Or — How the Other Half Lives
Nicholas Pashley.. 125

BEST QUOTES FROM FAMOUS CYNICS............................. 127

CARTOON
Larry Tyson... 128

The
CYNIC'S GUIDE
to Coping with Life

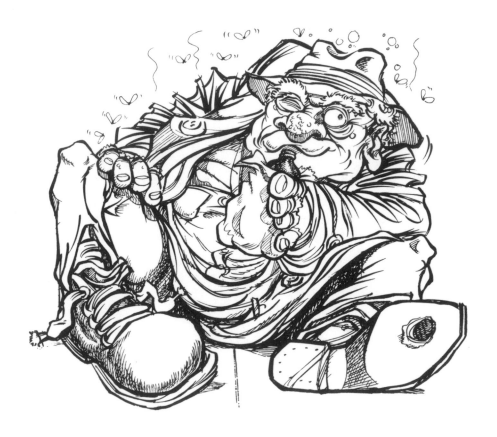

Cynic (circa 1956)

INTRODUCTION

The term cynic was once reserved for crusty old men who drank too much and looked at the world through a haze of cigarette smoke; their observations were tinged with contempt. But in this post-Aquarius age it has become not only fashionable, but necessary, to possess a healthy dose of cynicism to help you through the day.

The 1980s have become the decade of the churl. Successful careers have been built on the ability to sneer — David Letterman's for example. His meteoric rise to fame didn't rest solely on his lack of talent or the gap between his front teeth. No, it's his misanthropic views and sarcastic wit that keeps America awake until "Late Night." Even Walt Disney Studios, after sniffing this decade's prevailing winds, forced Jimminy Cricket into retirement and signed Bette Midler to a long-term contract.

It's not a pretty decade, and cynicism is just a healthy response to this world gone bad. Many people, in desperation, long nostalgically for the 1960s, when life had meaning and the music was good. But, cheer up. In future years, a generation that now thinks things *do* go better with coke will look back fondly on the 1980s. And this time the nostalgia will be for *us,* the uncelebrated heroes of our time: the cynics. And people will long to hear, once more, those voices that, with just the right amount of paranoia, declared "So what!"

WHAT'S POLLYANNA DONE LATELY?
Being a Cynic in the 1980s

These are not easy times for cynics. We are used to hearing, "Oh, don't be so cynical," whenever we comment realistically on the world as we see it. Have you noticed you don't hear that much any more?

Clearly, events have overtaken the cynic. In the world of Ronald Reagan, Oliver North, Chernobyl, AIDS, Gary Hart, and the PTL Club, it is difficult to take a stand that can raise eyebrows, even among the most naive of one's friends. When have you heard anyone suggest that maybe Ronald Reagan really *didn't* know about Iranscam, or that maybe Gary Hart actually *wasn't* sleeping with Donna Rice, or that just maybe there's an innocent explanation for all those missing PTL bucks? Even your maiden aunt — the one who still thinks Richard Pryor was the victim of an exploding rum and coke — has become jaded. Suddenly everyone's a cynic.

So it turns out we were right all along, we cynics. The world *was* a rotten place. People *were* lying to us. And we had been the only ones who knew it. People had called us crazy. "JFK's happily married to Jackie," they told us. "He wouldn't play around." Some people really believed that Rose Mary Woods had inadvertently erased those eighteen and a half minutes of tape. After all, she demonstrated how it could happen: you kept your foot on the button like so, and stretched like mad so your finger was on the other side of the room, and hey presto! You accidentally erased the tape. It could happen to anyone.

The Richard Nixon era was something of a watershed of modern cynicism. The genuine cynic knew that Nixon was a crook long before his team of third-rate gangsters bungled their break-in. Before we had even heard of the Watergate complex, *we* had seen through that shifty, shabby larcenist. Subsequent events showed us to have been unquestionably correct, and our numbers swelled. Yet even then, there were doubters. It was Gordon Liddy's fault. It was a momentary abberation. The president had fallen victim to an overzealous media campaign. It was just that particular president; the next one would be better. And, best of all: it showed that the system worked. After all, it took only a hostile Congress, a special prosecutor, months of Senate hearings, an inside informant, thousands of illicit tape recordings, countless subpoenas, round-the-clock work by numerous journalists, and a smoking gun to hound an obvious felon from office. And when it was all over, after billions of man-hours and dollars had been spent to prove what any decent cynic could have told them, they announced that the system worked. Anyone who disagreed was — you guessed it — a cynic.

Still, the Watergate circus added many new recruits to the cynics' team, as had the electoral demolition of George McGovern two years earlier. McGovern was the last significant effort of idealism and decency in American politics. After that, began the long slide to the institutionalized cynicism of the modern era.

And shouldn't we be happy, we survivors of all these wars? Shouldn't we rejoice to have swept all before us, to be able to say with pride that all men are now cynics? Can't we boast that surely even Mother Teresa must by now be one of us? Yes, and still . . . . There's still something niggling at us. Some fear, perhaps, that it's merely a trend like radicchio and Reeboks. Maybe it's that a lot of people have taken to cynicism just a tad too readily, without thinking it through. A feeling that by the time Vanna White's memoirs have been remaindered, optimism will once again spread through the land. Well, when it happens, there will still be a few of us, curmudgeonly to the end, crying out as we always have: "Oh you think so, do you?"

HOW TO COPE
WITH BEING ELVIS PRESLEY'S
LOVE CHILD

With the passing years, it appears that more and more of us are in fact the illegitimate children of Elvis Presley. Scientists have estimated that up to 85% of people born between late 1947 and May 1978 — the years between Presley's reaching puberty and the period covering nine months after his death — may actually be the Tupelo minstrel's offspring. Scarcely a day goes by, it seems, without another emotional mother declaring that yes, her child really was the product of her steamy romance with the greatest musician of this or any other age.

Such has been the flood of new claimants to the title of Elvis's love child that support groups have been established across North America and in many other countries, particularly West Germany, to help these unfortunate children — many of them grown adults by now — come to terms with their past. Social service agencies in the American south have been taxed to their limits attempting to deal with the problem, and emergency hotlines have been installed to assist confused young people in their need to know more.

All right, we hear you say, how do I know if I am Elvis's love child? First of all, were you born within the parameters mentioned above:

1947 to 1978? (Actually, Elvis was so unspeakably manly that he may have attained puberty well before the average age. In fact, this is almost certainly true. In addition, there have been many well-documented cases of Elvis reappearing after his death — sources as unimpeachable as Wayne Newton have confirmed this phenomenon — so it is not impossible that after-death conceptions might have taken place. So let's say, oh, between about 1938 and the present.)

If you can answer yes to the preceding question, ask yourself this one: are you noted for abominable taste in clothing and interior design? Take note that this does not confirm Elvis's paternity. There are lots of people totally unrelated to the Mississippi songbird who suffer from extremely bad taste. It does, however, seem likely that, if you find bespangled jumpsuits abhorrent, you are no child of Elvis.

Similarly, are you given, in ordinary conversation, to using expressions like "I was all shook up when I discovered my father was . . ." or "You know someone said the world's a stage and each must play a part," or even "I just want to be yo-hour te-heddy bear?" Do friends draw attention to your pelvis? Do you unconsciously surround yourself with burly yes-men? Is your idea of physical activity a game of touch football? (Be careful with this one — you could, in fact, be a Kennedy love child.) Are you otherwise bone-idle and completely aimless? Do you think of Las Vegas as a classy place? Yes? Then carry on.

Now we come to what for some is a touchy issue. Elvis, as we know, revered his mother. His mother was a saint. (Elvis shared this unusual status with his political mentor, Richard Nixon.) Your mother could never have tied Gladys Presley's shoelaces, so don't get uptight about the following questions. After all, experts have estimated that Elvis slept with some twenty-five million women in his short life, and, let's face it, your mother was no better than she had to be. All right, here goes:

1. Has your mother ever gone on a pilgrimage to Graceland?

2. Would your mother stay up late to watch a rerun of *Blue Hawaii*?

3. Does your mother think that Elvis's recording of *My Way* was a valid use of wax?

4. Was your mother a teenager in Germany in the fifties?

5. Was your mother ever a Vegas showgirl?

6. Was your mother an extra in *It Happened at the World's Fair*?

7. Was your mother a woman of child-bearing age in the U.S.A. or anywhere else in the known world between the dates mentioned above?

If you can answer yes to *any* of these questions, the chances are excellent that you are indeed Elvis's love child.

Now, having ascertained that your father was the King of Rock 'n' Roll, where do you go from here? First of all, you need legal advice. The Presley estate has a crew of sharp Philadelphia lawyers, so don't think you're going to mosy down to Memphis and take possession of Graceland. So far, it has to be said, your fellow half-siblings have proven unsuccessful at getting the estate to part with as much as a single single tasteless artifact from the great man's pleasure palace. This is discouraging, though it is worth noting that many of your putative half-brothers and -sisters are merely in it for the glory. Hard as it may be to believe, many of them don't care about the money. Don't make this mistake. Elvis was your father. What was his should be yours.

Can you sing at all? Take lessons. A flashy nightclub act will convince others of your rich musical heritage. This, of course, will put you in direct competition with the approximately fifteen thousand other entertainers across North America whose only source of income is earned through Elvis impersonation. Fewer than half of these, however, actually claim to be Elvis's love children, so you will automatically soar above much of the crowd simply on authenticity.

Be sincere at all times, particularly when dealing with the media. Refer humbly but frequently to "ma daddy" and make it sound as if you may have met him. Pretend publicly that you are not interested in money, though don't specifically say so. Don't badmouth your half-brothers and -sisters. Don't badmouth Colonel Tom Parker. Call people ma'am amd sir. Dye your hair black. Treat your lawyer with the respect a noble professional deserves, and don't question his bills. He is doing all he can for you, and he may make you rich. Even if he doesn't, you have the satisfaction of knowing that you have had the very best legal care and advice, and that no one could have done better for you. Perhaps it was your own fault. Did you ever think of that? Remember who got your dad out of the hoosegow in *Jailhouse Rock* — his lawyer. A hard-working professional who provides a valuable service to the community.

(This piece has been paid for by LICK — Lawyers for the Illegitimate Children of the King. Serving the needs of love children for more than a year now. Well, eight months, anyway. Call 1-800-PRE-SLEY. Call now. An operator is waiting for your call. Major credit cards accepted.)

WHAT DID THE PRESIDENT FORGET

And When Did He Forget It?

1913
Forgets basic potty rules.

1917
Forgets pledge of allegiance.

1919
Forgets capital of Nebraska for first time.

1920
Moves to Dixon, Ill. Forgets Tampico, Ill.

1923
Forgets infield fly rule for first time.

1924
Forgets Pythagorean theorem.

1928
Forgets head (not screwed on).

1931
Forgets words to Eureka College Fighting Song.

1936
Gets work as Cub play-by-play announcer. Forgets infield fly rule again.

1937
Moves to Hollywood. Forgets Dixon, Ill.

1938
Forgets lines.

1946
Forgets the Second World War.

1952
Forgets name of first wife.

1958
Forgets words to "Yabba-Dabba-Dabba-Dabba-Dabba-Dabba-Dabba
Said the Monkey to the Chimp."

1960
Forgets having been a Democrat.

1962
Forgets General Electric's most important product.

1966
Becomes Governor of California. Forgets blacks, native people,
Chicanos, women, poor people, Democrats, etc.

1973
Forgets which league Cubs are in.

1976
Seeks Republican presidential nomination. Forgets capital of Nebraska
again.

1980
Elected president. Forgets difference between Brazil and Bolivia.

1981
Forgets to duck.

1982
Forgets which ones are the Sandinistas and which ones are the Contras. Forgets own zip code. Forgets Nebraska altogether.

1983
Forgets briefly that his son is a ballet dancer.

1984
Forgets name of vice-president. Forgets Congress. Forgets the difference between Iran and Iraq.

1985
Forgets what he said in 1980 about Jimmy Carter's laughable Iran policy. Forgets that Iranians are Moslems, sends *Bible* to Tehran. Forgets Africa. Forgets Idaho. Forgets own address.

1986
Forgets difference between self and White House chief of staff; gets jumpy when Nancy demands Regan's dismissal. Forgets proper name for skin cancer, calls it "my little pal that I squoze." Forgets everything he's been told in countless boring meetings with Poindexter, Casey, Secord, McFarlane, Meese, Schultz, and that wacky Marine what-sisname. Forgets the bit in the oath of office about upholding the law. Forgets difference between Libya and Syria; bombs Libya because it's closer. Forgets name and sex of Princess of Wales, calls her Princess David at state banquet. Forgets distinction between self and animal kingdom, sends Christmas card to one-time colleague Bonzo.

1987
Forgets name of second wife. Forgets Canada, much of South America, and all of Australasia. Forgets Massachusetts, as well as Vermont, South Dakota, and the Carolinas. Forgets he didn't actually fight in the First World War. Forgets difference between surplus and deficit. Forgets old co-stars are mostly dead. Names Bonzo to Supreme Court.

LITTLE MISS PROFIT

Little Miss Profit
Leaned on her toffit
Soliciting her way
Along came a copper
Who threatened to stop her
So Miss Profit blew him
                      away

THERE WAS AN OLD MAN

There was an old man
Who sent arms to Iran
Then soon he quickly forgot
The press got a-hold
Of the story untold
But all was denied
(Though most likely he lied)
To keep from getting caught

GRUMPTY DUMPTY

Grumpty Dumpty sat on a wall
Grumpty Dumpty had a great fall
All of the day
And all through the night
He bitched!

COPING WITH CULTURE

How To Enjoy A Night At The Opera Even If The Marx Brothers Aren't In It

Certainly, there was a time when you wore nothing but blue jeans, and your idea of an evening out was a movie or rock concert. But you've changed. Well, for the sake of argument, let's say you've changed. You've become aware that there are other things out there. You want to become a little better rounded. You want to be a little more versatile. You no longer want to be a member of the great unwashed. Perhaps you've even started using deodorant.

Your campaign to better yourself has taken several predictable steps. You've been seen drinking imported beer. You've eaten Japanese food in public. You've attended a play or two, and in buildings that don't serve dinner before the first act and dessert at the intermission. You've seen *Amadeus* and had an opinion.

Good work! Now it's time to try the more difficult stuff. Ballet is useful, if a little effete. Too steady a diet of sushi and ballet can lead to irreversible social problems. Women, by and large, are much keener than men on ballet. This is easy to understand. Female ballet dancers tend to have enormous muscular thighs and no chests at all. Female ballet dancers are famous for their bones, for the good reason that you can see most of them. Terrific clavicles. This goes down well with the female ballet fans who, for some reason, all wish they looked like ballet dancers.

At the same time, male ballet dancers are inclined towards the muscular type. They have great legs and spectacular bottoms, which are regularly exposed in form-fitting tights. Many men find this phenomenon absurd and even distasteful, but are ill-advised to mention this at the time, lest they be labelled philistines. Men can be sure that their own bottoms will be compared, not at all favourably, with the leading man's later on. It will do you no good to observe that he's almost certainly gay, particularly if he is Mikhail Baryshnikov, who has fathered Jessica Lange's love child, which is more than you'll ever do.

Ballets have plots, which will be outlined in your program. The plots are silly and inconsequential, and usually have something to do with love, and often death. Sad ballets are about death; happy ballets are about love, or perhaps Christmas. The beginner need not worry unduly about the plot. The beginner will be too busy wondering who first came up with the idea of making people move in such a peculiar fashion. It is not easy to walk around like a ballet dancer. It takes literally years of practice, which makes one wonder even more why they bother.

Or you could try the opera. Opera these days is a booming growth industry, and you might want to get in on it before you're dismissed as a complete neanderthal. Opera is usually more expensive than ballet, and it almost always goes on longer, but you get a good class of people at the opera and it can do you no harm to be seen there.

The rap on opera used to be that the singers were all old and fat and hopelessly unbelievable as young romantic characters. That has changed to a great extent. A new breed of young soprano bombshells has made opera the spectator sport it deserves to be. Youthful superstars like Kathleen Battle, Carol Vaness, Frederica Von Stade (from New Jersey, no less), and the Kiwi songstress Kiri te Kanawa are all knockouts and sing like bejeezus to boot. They can drop by my place to gargle any time they like.

The men, unfortunately, still lean a bit towards bulk. Pavarotti, of course, is the size of a house. Placido Domingo looks lithe by comparison, but you'd still want him to keep his shirt on. Fortunately, opera designers resist the temptation to dress their tenors in tights, but it is easy to see why women prefer ballet.

Operas have plots the way Ronald Reagan has polyps. They just never quit. The plots are difficult to follow, in part because the singers are singing in a foreign language. Even if they sing in English, you can't make out most of it anyway, which is just as well. You'd only find the words insufferably silly. There are dozens of books available to tell you what the opera you're going to see is about. No one has ever managed to finish a plot outline, but you can get a rough idea of who's who.

Take a well-known opera like the Italian comic masterpiece *Acqua Minerale* by San Pellegrino. The title is difficult to translate precisely; the opera is generally known in English as "They (f.) Do Things Like This All The Time, But At The End Of The Day We (m.) Love Them To Little Bits, The Cunning Little Vixens."

The action takes place in the Italian town of Ferraro. After the sprightly overture, the curtain opens to reveal a merry band of peasants, who sing the jolly chorus "La-La-La-La-La" ("Here we all are having a particularly good time; what care we about tomorrow?"). They exit to lukewarm applause, waving garlands over their heads. Enter Geraldine, who sings the wistful *"Ho perduta il treno"* ("I could have been a contender, but this gang of whoreson dogs have spoiled my happiness").

Enter Garagiola, the leader of the street gang *(I Republicani)* that has discredited Geraldine by exposing the shady financial practices of Gianni, her betrothed. He sings the famous aria *"Ah, che questo raggagga a un bello seno"* ("I have always fancied my chances with this little bit of fluff"), then the two sing the duet *"Vest la giubba"* ("The chubby one has a nice waistcoat").

Enter Gianni, Geraldine's beloved, followed by *I Tax Inspectori* (The Tax Inspectors). Unfortunately the night you are there, the well-known Paraguayan tenor who was going to sing the role of Gianni is indisposed. Actually, he has been held up in Finland by an air traffic controllers' strike. Luckily his place has been taken at the last moment by Hans Drang, the great German tenor, whose gig in Thailand has been cancelled, owing to an outbreak of legionnaire's disease at the Bangkok Opera House. Unfortunately, Drang is not familiar with the role of Gianni, being a German tenor, so he will sing instead the role of Waldheim from Wagner's immortal opera *"Lowenbrau."*

So, enter Waldheim. He sings *"Ich bin nicht ein Nazi"* ("I was not where they said I was, I did none of those things they said I did, anyway you had to follow orders in those difficult times, can't we put the past behind us?"). As chance would have it, this aria is similar in theme to Gianni's *"Non sono mafioso"* ("I was not where they said I was, I did none of the things they said I did, it's just the way things are done in Queens"). Waldheim, Geraldine, and Garagiola sing the great trio *"La donna e mobile"* ("Madonna's doing a world tour to promote her new record"), and Waldheim is led off in chains. The chorus reenters and sings the charming "Mairzy doats and doazy doats" and the first act is over, so get to the bar right away if you plan to throw back a couple of quick belts before Act 2.

And so it goes. There will be an alto called Donna Somebody, and a trio of interfering busybodies all called Don Something — probably Alfredo, Bolognese, and Pesto. There will be a pert servant girl who knows more than she lets on, and there may — if you're very unlucky — be somebody who is actually of a different sex than the character she's playing. Acts 2, 3, and 4 will unfold in a confusing manner, and the entire evening will be a long one. Long for you and long for the singers, who all woke up in different cities this morning — Geraldine in Prague, Waldheim in Montevideo, and Garagiola in Sydney. Tomorrow night, Geraldine will be performing Bellini's *Baloney* in Bologna, Waldeim stars in Donizetti's *Donna Rice* at Disneyworld, and Garagiola will be doing the "Game of the Week" from Fenway Park. The globe-trotting nature of modern opera will take its toll in Act 3, when Geraldine breaks into *"Quella opera e la questo?"* ("Excuse me, is this Covent Garden?") from Luigi's *Trattoria*, and again in Act 4, when she does her famous death scene.

As always her death scene is tremendously moving. Unfortunately, this opera does not have a death scene. Comic operas always end with justice prevailing (in this case, Geraldine and Gianni are vindicated and *I Republicani* are defeated); tragic operas end with the soprano dying of the Soprano Syndrome. The Soprano Syndrome is a disease rather like the one that claimed Ali McGraw in *Love Story*. It leaves the sufferer looking, if anything, healthier than in the first act. There are no unsightly marks and no visible loss of either weight or hair. It permits the patient to sing almost uninterruptedly throughout the final scene — in fact, right up to the moment of her demise at centre stage. It is followed by the final curtain and prolonged applause.

And here's where you come in. To impress with your knowledge of opera, find out beforehand which of the singers is the most famous. Check your program to find out which one it is, and wait for your moment, either immediately after a blockbuster aria or during the curtain calls. Opera is one of the few art forms in which you get to shout. In this respect, it's a bit like a ballgame, although so far the Wave has not come into vogue in the major opera houses.

If you're feeling particularly testy, you can actually boo. Try this only at the Met or La Scala. This is a risky procedure, as you might have to justify your strong opinion, and you'll wind up muttering something about the singer's questionable coloratura in the third act quartet and exposing yourself as a fraud.

Or you can cheer. At the opera house, "Hooray!" or "Good on ya, ya little beauty!" are still frowned upon, even in these democratic days. "Bravo!" remains the old standby. But there are perils here as well, and the beginner can find himself committing a *faux pas* of the worst sort. "Bravo!" is fine for a male singer, but a female singer requires "Brava!" If you're mad about the whole gang of singers you need "Bravi!" unless it's all women, like the Rhine Maidens or the Ladies of the Night, in which case it's "Brave!" pronounced a bit like Ave in *"Ave Maria."*

With a bit of work you too can become an opera buff. You will understand the jokes in the intermission blather on the "Live at the Met" broadcasts. You will learn to tell Siegfried from Sieglinde. You will learn to call Beverly Sills "Bubbles." You will overcome all obstacles and will ascend to Valhalla.

SNOBS...

ABS, WELL DEFINED,
PECS, HARD AS
CREOSOTE,
LATS, OUTSTANDING,
... WOULDN'T YOU
SAY,
PORKY?...

AN AMUSING
LITTLE
VINTAGE,
IT HAS A CERTAIN
Je ne sais quoi...
AND HOW IS
YOUR
DR. PEPPER?

MY INCOME
MAY BE
$ 300 A YEAR,
BUT I'M A
CREATIVE
ARTIST!

BODYBUILDERS   WINE BUFFS   POETS

COPING WITH SNOBS

You need never feel belittled by superior sorts again. When talked down to, simply resort to the leveling phrase . . . .

COPING WITH LOVE GODDESSES OF THE EIGHTIES
Bad Girls of Our Time

More than any era in recent memory, the eighties have produced a new super breed of bad girls. Seldom have men — poor weak souls that they are — been at the mercy of such skilled temptresses. Who are these modern courtesans, these practiced wreckers of homes, careers, and multi-million-dollar enterprises? And who are the men who fall prey to these sultry love goddesses?

Step forward, Ms. Donna Rice. Like many a seductress before her, Donna Rice has operated as a "model" and "actress," all the better to provide a legitimate excuse for parading about with next to nothing on. Veteran observers of Ms. Rice have noted that at some point in her career as a "model" her bust increased significantly in size. This sudden alteration may have resulted from a successful exercise program; alternatively, it may bear the trademark of modern technology. Whatever the case, only a fool would deny the obvious "charms" of this Miami mademoiselle, particularly in a skimpy bathing costume. Her physical appeal, coupled with what I am certain is a winning personality, has made her a young woman of considerable appeal on a global level. She has been linked "romantically" with pop star Don

Henley, Prince Albert of Monaco, and international gunrunner Adnan Khashoggi.

What really put Ms. Rice on the map, of course, was her well-publicized failure to sleep with presidential frontrunner Gary Hart. She spent at least two weekends — one on a boat called *Monkey Business*, another in a Washington townhouse — in close proximity to Senator Hart, but not apparently sleeping with him. Both parties to these non-encounters have been quite clear on the matter. This failure to consummate his "friendship" with Ms. Rice led Mr. Hart to withdraw from the presidential race out of severe embarrassment. His wife has been more than supportive of Mr. Hart through these difficulties, but the damage has been done.

Jessica Hahn, on the other hand, did go to bed with Jim Bakker. This is a fact. In a rare case of openness, both parties involved have confirmed that acts of a sexual nature took place in the Sheraton Sand Key Hotel in Florida. Beyond these basic facts, however, the stories diverge. Ms. Hahn, a youthful church secretary, claims to have been of a chaste disposition at the time of her adventure, while Mr. Bakker — a man of good character and significant personal wealth — insists that Ms. Hahn was sophisticated in the ways of love, a regular little Jezebel in fact. Given the Reverend Mr. Bakker's track record of clean thoughts and good deeds, it is safe to say that his version is the true one, and that he was led off the straight and narrow path by a scheming bawd who was not above taking $115,000 of the Lord's money to stay silent about the affair.

It is also worth noting that Mr. Bakker — a righteous and Godly man — was driven to this single act of passion by the behaviour of his worldy wife Tammy Faye, a singer of religious tunes who, at the time of her husband's moment of indiscretion, was enjoying all-night "recording sessions" with the creater of "Alley Oop" and "The Monster Mash." When we are casting the first stone, it is hard to determine which of these Delilahs should be the target. Between them, they have brought a good man down.

Then there is the case of Romina Danielson, a hussy if ever there was one. Donna and Gary both denied their story. Jessica and Jim both admitted theirs. Romina Danielson and Peter Holm can't agree on anything. Did they or didn't they? Remember the old days when men boasted about their sexual adventures and women kept quiet about them? Well, that's all changed now. The torrid Romina, another "actress," it is worth noting, testified in a court of law that she had frequent sexual encounters with former Swedish pop star Peter Holm at the mansion he shared with his wife, "actress" Joan Collins. Ms. Danielson reported that Mr. Holm graced her with the affectionate name of Passion Flower. So convincing did she find her own testimony that she fainted dead away and was carried out of the courtroom screaming.

Mr. Holm, with a dignity acquired from his years in the Stockholm pop music *demi-monde*, denied Ms. Danielson's tales vehemently. And rightly so. Ms. Collins, comely still at 54, hardly needs to sit in a Los Angeles courtroom and listen to some shapely strumpet who's young enough to be her daughter tell the world about copulating with her husband. Any respectable husband would deny the story, rather than humiliate his loving wife. But did it do Peter Holm any good? Did he earn the undying gratitude of his thespian helpmeet? Hah! He was thrown out into the street, chucked out of the marital home, with scarcely a penny to his name, reduced to begging the courts for a meagre settlement. A man can learn a lesson from the sad story of Peter Holm. Avoid "actresses."

Now, is Fawn Hall a bad girl? She certainly looks the type. She has worked as a "model," though not, as far as we know, as an "actress." Tall and sultry, Ms. Hall is the sort of secretary that cartoonists have built careers on. So what if she made the odd typing error? So what if she accidentally put $8 million into the Swiss bank account of the Sultan of Brunei? Hubba hubba! You can always find someone who types. A world-class shredder is something much rarer. And talk about devotion to her job! Ms. Hall was prepared to mar her perfect figure by packing troublesome documents into her foundation garments and smuggling them out of the office.

But did Fawn Hall sleep with her boss, Lt-Col. Oliver North? In sworn testimony, Ollie North said no. Can he be believed? After all, his wife was sitting right behind him. Of his televised testimony before a congressional committee, some 62% of Americans reported that they believed he was telling the truth when he said he had been lying previously. (A further 28% thought he might have been telling the truth earlier and lying now. The remaining 10% think he's been lying all along and shows no signs of changing.)

Is Ollie North telling the truth about Fawn Hall? If you think that everything he says is a lie, then he definitely slept with her. Otherwise, maybe he didn't. We know she was sleeping with Arturo Cruz Jr., son of Arturo Cruz Sr., a leading Contra. Does that make her a bad girl? It may depend on your politics. Perhaps it is too early to say for sure. We know that Ollie North was fired from his job at the White House, which, as we have seen from earlier cases, is usually a surefire sign.

Finally, Vanna White. Is Vanna White a bad girl? Definitely not. Vanna White is everything that's good about American womanhood. Vanna White is a paragon. If all women were like Vanna White, Gary Hart would be on his way to the White House, Jim Bakker would be at the helm of the PTL Club, and Peter Holm would be the toast of Uppsala today.

THE TEN COMMANDMENTS OF THE TRENDY

1. I am the Almighty Buck. Thou shalt have no goals before me.

2. Remember thy pocket pager and keep it handy.

3. Thou shalt not take the name of thy BMW mechanic in vain.

4. Honor thy analyst and thy aerobics instructor.

5. Thou shalt dress to kill (and thou shalt choose the right accessories).

6. Thou shalt drink imported beer.

7. Thou shalt not wear street shoes on the squash court.

8. Thou shalt not admit to watching "Muppet Babies."

9. Thou shalt not covet thy neighbor's RRSP.

10. Thou shalt not covet thy neighbor's divorce settlement.

The Four Horsemen of the Apocalypse — Pestilence, Famine, War and Death — are the front runners in the human misery sweepstakes. But let's not forget the minor miseries, pet peeves and pains-in-the-butt. These are:

THE HORSEMEN OF THE PETTY ANNOYANCE

A LISTENER'S GUIDE TO CONTEMPORARY RADIO

Remember what radio used to be like? Well, it's all changed now. Nowadays, there is a radio station designed for every sort of listener. We read in the papers about the new categories of programming, but do we understand all the terms? How do we find a radio station that's right for us in this incredible spectrum of possibilities? It's not easy, but we've compiled a useful guide of the terms used and their target audiences, suitable for clipping. You should find no difficulty in locating the appropriate station in your area.

Adult Oriented Rock (AOR)

Target audience: listeners between 35 and 42. Programming: Lionel Ritchie, Kenny Rogers, Madonna, Phil Collins, Elton John, Michael Jackson, Paul Simon, Paul McCartney, Whitney Houston, George Michael, Dan Fogelberg.

Contemporary Adult Pop (CAP)

Target audience: listeners between 34 and 41. Programming: Madonna, Michael Jackson, George Michael, Phil Collins, Paul Simon, Elton John, Whitney Houston, Lionel Ritchie, Paul McCartney, Kenny Rogers, Dan Fogelberg.

Socially Aware Forty-Year-Old Environment (SAFE)

Target audience: listeners between 36 and 43. Programming: Paul Simon, Paul McCartney, Whitney Houston, Phil Collins, Elton John, Michael Jackson, George Michael, Madonna, Kenny Rogers, Dan Fogelberg.

Hip Aging Rock/Pop (HARP)

Target audience: listeners between 33 and 41. Programming: Whitney Houston, George Michael, Paul Simon, Phil Collins, Madonna, Paul McCartney, Lionel Ritchie, Elton John, Michael Jackson, Kenny Rogers, Dan Fogelberg.

Middle Of the Road Or Nothing (MORON)

Target audience: listeners in their 30s or 40s who sleep a lot. Programming: Dan Fogelberg, Kenny Rogers, Phil Collins, Lionel Ritchie, Michael Jackson, Whitney Houston, Madonna, George Michael, Paul McCartney, Elton John, Paul Simon.

Rock for Young Fogeys (RYF)

Target audience: people in their 20s who work in offices. Programming: Madonna, Whitney Houston, George Michael, Michael Jackson, Lionel Ritchie, Elton John, Paul Simon, Phil Collins, Kenny Rogers, Paul McCartney, Dan Fogelberg.

E-Z Listening (EZZZZZZZL)

Target audience: people in elevators or dentists' offices, also dead people. Programming: instrumental versions of songs by Kenny Rogers, Dan Fogelberg, Michael Jackson, Elton John, Phil Collins, Lionel Ritchie, Paul McCartney, Madonna, George Michael, Paul Simon, Whitney Houston.

Music Of Someone Else's Life (MOSEL)

Target audience: people who have been turned off by all this modern stuff they hear on other stations. Programming: The Beatles, Simon and Garfunkel, Kenny Rogers and the First Edition, the Commodores, Elton John, the Jackson Five, Dan Fogelberg, Wham, Genesis, Whitney Houston, Madonna.

YOU KNOW IT'S GOING TO BE 'ONE OF THOSE DAYS,' WHEN:

You find the 'Tidy Bowl Man' floating face down.

Your parrot starts saying 'I'll get back to you.'

The pervert who calls regularly, telephones collect from Hawaii where he is vacationing.

The baby suddenly takes to calling the postman 'Daddy.'

Guys that look like Mel Gibson start calling you 'Ma'am.'

You get complimented on your patterned stockings, but you aren't wearing any.

The news report announces 'sporadic gunfire' and 'enforced street curfew' on the island you've just booked for a two-week holiday.

Your 'Roach Motel' puts out a no vacancy sign.

The insurance salesman from next door drops by to borrow a cup of sugar, and asks casually "Have you ever considered annuities?"

The rasping cough you faked to call in sick won't go away.

The automatic banking machine wishes you a Merry Christmas, and it's June.

You are directed to the 'self-serve' line at the blood donor clinic.

You are notified that you have won third prize in absentia at an Ernest Borgnine lookalike contest.

IT'S IN THE STARS
Coping with
the New Astrology

If you were born on a day of the week, you can get ahead in this madcap world. Take a look at your sun signs — there could be big bucks on the horizon. Your rising sign could be a dollar sign. So, read on.

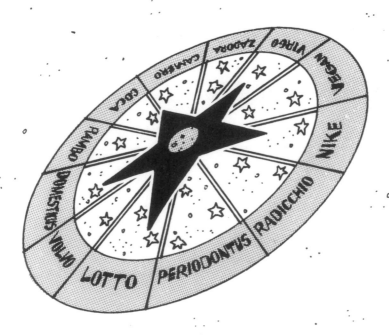

DOMESTICUS, The Realtor
(March 21—April 15)

If you were born under the sign of the realtor, you are likely enjoying an unprecedented run of success. You get on well with people and can find something good to say in the dingiest of surroundings. You try to look on the bright side. Where someone else sees a "swamp," you see "elegant waterside frontage." You are occasionally accused of insincerity by sourpusses. To hell with them. Don't tell them about the roof.

VOLVO, The Import
(April 16—May 8)

Those fortunate enough to have been born under Volvo can expect a smooth ride through a life filled with optional extras. You will have a child, perhaps two, who will be blessed with all the advantages you imagine yourself to have missed, including cute but somehow stuffy names. You will admire these children more than your friends do. The trust fund you have established in their names will make them richer than you. It will not make them more pleasant, however. Perhaps they will move far away.

CANCER, The Killer
(May 9—May 29)

Not a great sign, quite frankly. Especially nowadays, as everyone will whisper behind your back that you really have AIDS. Looking on the bright side, your dependents will collect big on your insurance policies. Congratulations! You have beaten the system. In a way.

LOTTO, The Gambler
(May 30—noon, June 20)

You have a keen interest in numbers, as well as an irrational notion that some particular numbers are somehow luckier for you than others, despite all the evidence to the contrary. One Lottarian in a million (or so) will come into great wealth, but will make idiotic statements to the press to the effect that he or she will not be changed by this sudden change of fortune. Old friends will change toward the lucky Lottarian, usually because they will no longer live in the same neighbourhood.

PERIODONTUS, The Giver of Pain
(12:01 p.m. June 20—July 13)

These are good times for those born under this sign. An ever-growing population is entering the prime gum-disease years. Where you used to make a lousy 25 bucks for giving some guy a filling, you can now get ten times that by setting some 16-year-old out of dental hygiene college loose on the same guy while you put your feet up. Let the others work hard. They'll all come to you eventually.

RADICCHIO, The New Leaf
(July 14—August 12)

Another sign in its ascendancy. You are crisp and popular, and très, très chic. You are seen in the best places. There are those who accuse you of bitterness, but you don't give a toss. And why should you? You're enjoying your salad days.

NIKE, The Runner
(August 13—September 1)

Those born under the sign of Nike will go the distance. Also known as The Shin Splint, Nike rules the lower limbs. Nikeans love to travel. Boston and New York could be in your future. Knee problems may trouble you. Take them as a message from nature, and relax, for Pete's sake. And don't talk about it; no one wants to hear.

LOTHARIO, The Hart
(September 2—September18)

Lotharians are notorious for their hopeless attraction to the opposite sex. In these troubled times, with both disease and puritanism ascendant, Lothario is in something of a decline. Those born under this sign live for pleasure, and should not be surprised at the resentment of others. This is not a good time for Lotharians to run for president or attempt to run a TV ministry.

VEGAN, The Spurner of Meat
(September 19—October 14)

Sometimes known as Tofu, Vegan is the sign of the abstemious and the thin-blooded. Vegans find they are not invited for dinner twice, for some reason. Your lucky flower is the lentil, and much joy may it bring you. Vegans should try not to sigh obnoxiously when others order a rare steak. If God had meant us not to eat meat, he wouldn't have made cows fat and easy to catch.

VIRGO, The Celibate
(October 15—November 21)

During the sixties and seventies, this sign virtually disappeared from the astrological calender, but the eighties have witnessed a remarkable recovery, and the sign now occupies more than a full month. In the years 1981 and 1982, every women's magazine in North America featured articles on The New Celibacy ("Celibacy Saved My Marriage," that sort of thing). The phenomenon was at first regarded as a joke, but AIDS and careers have legitimized it and made it a way of life for millions. Virgos scarcely need mates, but if they did, they could find them among Nikes, Vegans, and Radicchians. Avoid Lotharians.

ZADORA, The Bimbo
(Nov. 22—Dec.14)

Marry money.

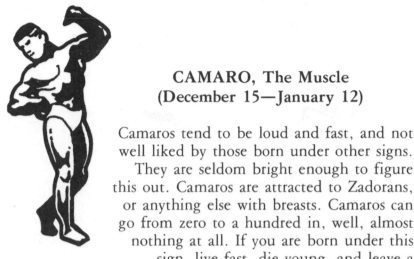

CAMARO, The Muscle
(December 15—January 12)

Camaros tend to be loud and fast, and not well liked by those born under other signs. They are seldom bright enough to figure this out. Camaros are attracted to Zadorans, or anything else with breasts. Camaros can go from zero to a hundred in, well, almost nothing at all. If you are born under this sign, live fast, die young, and leave a beautiful corpse. Soon.

COCA, The Old Leaf
(January 13—February 25, or whatever)

Those born under the sign of Coca are often martyrs to sinus problems and may frequently need to have their wallets drained. Cocans are to be found in the company of baseball players and rock musicians, and less pleasant company it's difficult to imagine. You may have been born with a golden spoon around your neck, but don't let the commissioner find out or you will have to appear in public mouthing platitudes.

RAMBO, The Hero
(Feb. 26—March 20)

This is a difficult sign to be sure about. People born under this sign are inclined to follow orders, but they may be the teeniest bit easy-going in interpreting said orders. There's a lot of luck involved here. If your name is, say, William Calley, you might become an embarrassment to your country. If, on the other hand, your name is Ollie North, you can lie to Congress, shred documents of national interest, and run naked in the streets brandishing a gun, and people will urge you to run for president. Go figure.

COPING WITH INTROSPECTION

We've all been subjected, at one time or another, to the harangues of others when it comes to self-analysis. You are what you eat, what you drive, what you earn — the list is endless. We all know, of course, that in fact you are what you think — or at least what people think you think. So it is important to choose a personal philosophy that you can live by, but which also establishes your status amongst your friends and acquaintances.

It is especially important that you appear to change with the times; no one likes a has-been. So don't talk in public about such things as the sexual revolution. It's long been over, and sex lost. Old ideas are like old suits; at first they're just comfortable to slip into, but they soon get threadbare, and it is not long before people can see right through them to the real you. This is something that you will want to avoid.

So, how do you choose a personal philosphy that's right for you? First of all you must cast aside any reservations that you might have, especially if it's been several years since you substantially changed your outlook. Reservations, as some wag once said, are the dutch caps in the birth of new ideas. Nor must you allow stodgy or academic friends to persuade you to take night courses in arcane and obscure subjects. These will just frustrate you. The point of academic philosophy is to produce concepts and allusions to puzzle and worry us, and to convince us that we are incorrigibly ignorant and that the world should be run by small, bearded, teutonic college professors who can exist on great thoughts alone, coupled with occasional emotional support provided by female students, preferably under the age of twenty-one. Shop around a bit; try a few ideas on for size in the privacy of your own home. See how they feel.

If you're the unadventurous type, why not go for the tried and true — the Freudian view? However, if you *do* decide to adopt a Freudian outlook on life, you should be very careful of the very next thing you do. This will be a *primary action*, which will cause your subconscious to conjure up a *secondary reaction*, which then leads to a permanent fixation. For instance, if the first thing you do after becoming a disciple of Freud is eat a meal, then you will be condemned to a life of feeling hungry whenever you feel you should eat a meal. You can see where bad habits of this kind can lead. Inevitably you will become an incurable pervert with intermittent periods of neurotic conflict — as, indeed, did Freud.

Then there's Carl Jung, the second-largest export from Switzerland after the cuckoo clock. One of the great advantages of being a Jungian is that you can get all your introspection done in your sleep, reserving your daylight hours for wage-earning, laundry, doing lunch etc. Jung tells you that your dreams reveal tremendously significant things about your repressed self (hatred of your grandmother, male siblings, and neighbours, to name but a few), and if you can analyze your dream symbols you can find out just who you can't stand and why. If you can't translate these symbols into everyday experiences, then you are not dreaming them properly. Unlike the Freudians, however, the Jungians will not take this personally, and you will be allowed to go on having symbolic dreams until you get them right. In the eventual outcome, you will come to the realization that you aren't really you at all, but a piece of someone else who is much bigger than you are, which goes a long way to cutting back on your responsibilities.

If you'd rather go in for one of the hard-core philosophies, you can choose between idealism, communism, Lamarckism, and that big downer, existentialism, all of which are the domains of intractable teutons with names you can't pronounce, let alone spell. They are also frighteningly close to academic "subjects," and may come with course numbers, homework, tests, and papers — all of which you grew out of years ago.

And that leaves spiritualism. Make no mistake about it, since the publication of Shirley Maclaine's last three books, spiritualism has really come into its own, and the universe as we know it will never be the same. From the moment that Shirley confessed that she had taken a trip to the moon on a gossamer-thin silver thread, great thinkers have had to admit that the very foundations of scientific and philosophic theory have crumbled before our incredulous eyes. Because of Shirley, formerly reluctant mediums are now coming forward and admitting that they are really human radio through which people who were reticent and dull-witted during the time that they were alive are at last able to give spiritual guidance to top stars now that they are dead.

One follower of Shirley's claims to use a bizarre, crystal safety-deposit box — crafted by aliens untold centuries ago, and thought to be one of only eighty-seven in existence in the California area — to pick up the essential vibes of Hollywood's glitterati. In fact, spiritualism has become so popular that people are just walking off the street and into the prestigious California Institute of Spending Large Amounts of Money on Embarrassing Ideas, claiming to be "paranormal" (heterosexual members of armed airborne divisions). Scientists have even gone so far as to postulate that the rings around Saturn are, in fact, made up of billions of copies of *Out On A Limb*, discarded by people who have achieved nirvana.

If none of these philosophic choices appeal to you, then you can always show that you're an open-minded and prophetic thinker by simply choosing a concept that vaguely appeals, then prefix it with neo- (you should avoid doing this with the word Nazi, unless you are an Austrian head of state). "Neo-Freudianism" is good if you want to talk about your libido in public places without the punitive repercussions that come with the real thing.

If, however, after an exhausting session of introspection, you find that you have been unable to find unanswerable proof of your existence, let alone an underlying meaning for it, and you don't care any more what friends and acquaintances think of your mind, then ask yourself the question first posed by the twentieth-century American philosopher, Bette Midler; "Why bother?"

Coping with Other People's Bad Habits Department

GREAT MOMENTS
IN THE HISTORY OF
NON-SMOKING

The Winston-Salem War-On-Smoking Crimes Trial: 1985.
Seated in the prisoner's dock, left to right (back row) Alfred Dunhill,
John Player-Special, Winston Cools, Richard Virginia Slims.
(Front row) Adolph Marlboro, James T. Camel and Billy-Bob 'Lucky' Strike.

King Cough: 1984. The anti-smoking lobby financed
a remake of this '30s classic.

1979: The International Non-Smoking Expedition conquers Everest and declares it a no-smoking zone.

Pope John Paul II lectures the faithful on the evils of smoking.

COPING WITH MEN
A Beginner's Guide for Women

Modern women are divided on the subject of men. Some are all for 'em, others dead against 'em. Still, love them or hate them, there are close to 2.5 billion men alive on this planet as we go to press, so some measure of coexistence seems inevitable. Let's take a look at men. Let's see who they are and what makes them tick.

Even in this relatively sensible era, there are women who feel all at sea without a man in their lives. Why this should be so is a mystery. It is possibly best explained as a throwback to the early years of human evolution when women needed something big and stupid to kill mammoths and sabre-toothed tigers. As a species, we have developed to the point where men are now needed merely to kill spiders and understand plumbing (and sometimes not even then). Yet they have managed to thrive where other useless creatures have vanished from the food chain altogether.

The survival of men into this century has been the result of unduly generous treatment by women. Women have coddled men and shielded them from the worst of life's hardships. Behind every great man, we are told, stands an even greater woman, very often propping

the fellow up on her shoulders. Yet until very recently, these same men forbade women to vote. Women were — and in some areas still are — regarded as property.

Where do they get off, these men? Let's try to understand them, as vile a prospect as that may be. Men are, on average, bigger than women. They tend to be ungainly and ill-proportioned. They grow hair in inappropriate places and often fail to grow it where it would suit them best. Their dress sense is, at best, primitive. Their interest in personal hygiene is all too often entirely lacking, and they revel in producing smells and noises of a barnyard character. Their failure to evolve significantly from the mammoth-hunting days leads to an aggressiveness that is almost invariably misdirected and self-destructive. Similarly their lust for red meat shortens their lives and leads to bizarre, anachronistic practices like hunting. Even relatively intelligent men — university graduates and leaders of large corporations — can, to this day, be heard describing a basic green salad as "rabbit food."

While the male brain is fairly well-developed in many cases, its use is far too frequently diverted into totally useless directions. Some 65% of North American men can (and will) tell you Ty Cobb's lifetime batting average, although this knowledge has never been proven useful to a single one of them. (Ty Cobb was a particularly unpleasant baseball player of the first half of this century. He was a racist and sexist monster, known to drink to excess and abuse firearms. The relatively benign "Babe" Ruth, on the other hand, was merely a loud-mouthed, gin-soaked philanderer. More than 50 years after either of these "giants" of the game last played, grown men who claim at least to understand both nuclear fission and non-sexist child-rearing continue to debate the relative merits of these two long-dead cavemen.)

Modern men frequently claim to have feelings. They particularly claim to possess feelings of a tender sort towards women. Unfortunately, they frequently claim to possess these feelings towards several women in the same town at the same time. Perhaps there is a male dog that runs loose in your neighbourhood. You may see this dog sniffing about after every female dog (usually called bitches — and what does that tell you about men and language?) in the vicinity, urinating wherever he pleases, and keeping neighbours awake with nocturnal howling. The average man is a lot like that stray dog. Like any successful dog, the average man is capable of begging pitifully, then turning on you and snapping viciously. Unfortunately, it is woman's tragic flaw to be smitten by apparently helpless creatures like dogs, cats, and men. The intelligent woman knows better than to expect gratitude from any of these dumb creatures.

Yet the old ways persist, and women still feel some primeval need for a man. Much of this stems from social pressure. And certainly a good marriage can bring with it the great comforts of life, including microwave ovens, central air conditioning, and other major human needs. Clearly, it is still the case that men — the great hunters — usually earn (or at least *make*) more money than women, so there are financial advantages to a good marriage. Conversely, there can be nothing that better illustrates the notion that women are inherently masochistic than the sight of a woman marrying a man who earns less than she does.

We are told at regular intervals that men in today's society are hard to come by. There are reasons for this. Approximately half of today's men are inexplicably gay all of a sudden. (And if you seek further proof of the tom-cat nature of men, look at what happens to men who cut themselves off from the civilizing influence of women. If women went to bathhouses, for instance, they would bathe.) Of the rest, many have been killed or seriously maimed in masculine pursuits such as war, gang combat, organized sports, fast driving, or early death brought on by booze and fatty foods.

This shortage of men should, of course, be something for women to applaud. If heterosexual men become any more scarce, perhaps there will be intelligent television programming on weekends. Yet the popular magazines remind us that women are growing more and more concerned about their ability to attract one of the handful of un-attached, fairly presentable, heterosexual, HRV-negative men still out there. Without raising once again the question of why they want one, let us see what these women need to do to land one of these in-creasingly rare specimens.

The secret boils down to what experts call the "button" technique. In a nutshell, this formula says "Button up your brain, unbutton your blouse." The first part of the technique calls for you to suppress your natural intelligence and feign an interest in the man and his aesthetically bankrupt life. Listen to him go on about his hopeless job and his football team and the pack of losers he went to high school with, and you're well on the way. The second part is self-explanatory. Men are interested in only one thing . . . actually this is not true. They are interested in many things — cars, sports, their jobs, party politics — but they are easily distracted. Make him think you're interested in the hilarious caper he got up to in high school, then get him gawking at your bosom, and you've just about got him. What you do with him then, quite frankly, is up to you.

COPING WITH THE OPPOSITE SEX
Things to Avoid in a Mate

To avoid having to endure a lifetime of coping with an ill-considered spouse's little peccadillos, choose wisely. It is suggested ending a relationship after the first date in the case of:

A Man Who
- says his favourite actor is Mr. T

- wears platform shoes on the beach

- boasts he can braid the hair on his back

- wears hand-made braces on his teeth

- can lick his eyebrows

- last dated his sister

- can belch "Moonlight Sonata"

- enrolled in Parking Lot Attendant school, but failed

- counts ketchup as a vegetable

- can whistle using his fingers, *and* his toes

- favourite colour is plaid

- moves his lips when reading comic books

- laughs out loud at "The Brady Bunch"

- wears hat size 4 1/4

A Woman Who
- buys her make-up at 7-Eleven

- wears orthopaedic halter tops

- types 85 words a minute, but thinks 3

- can't wait for *Friday the 13th, Part VII*

- spayed her cat herself

- once won a Tammy Fae Bakker lookalike contest

- is a dental hygienist in an AIDS clinic

- gets Thank You cards from motorcycle gangs

- has been vaccinated against distemper

- makes her own jewelry out of coathangers and bottle caps

- likes to hang around poorly-lit underground parking garages at night

- favourite book is *TV Guide*

- ex-boyfriend is out on parole

- is listed under 'accessories' in Corvette manuals

- put her sister through college on the deposits from her empties

- gets a bulk discount from the electrolysist

COPING WITH WOMEN
A Beginner's Guide for Men

Can't live with them, can't live without them. That's the book on women. Formerly known as girls, chicks, dames, or broads, women have really come into their own in the last two decades. Areas that were once regarded as exclusively male domains have been forced to open their doors to women — areas like heart disease and lung cancer, for instance. For the first time in generations, the actuary's gender gap is actually beginning to close. Formerly women died only when the deceased husband's funds ran out.

Funny people, women. Freud asked, "What do women want?" and we're still trying to find out. Do they want Sylvester Stallone or Alan Alda? They won't give us a definite answer. Whichever one they wind up with, they get wistful about the other. They marry a guy for his mind, they want him to be good at home repairs. They marry a guy for his pectorals, they want him to talk about art. They marry a guy who's sensitive, they get mad he doesn't earn more. They marry a rich guy who can give them the creature comforts, they complain that he's at the office all the time, then they run off with the gardener.

Women are romantic, right? It's a known fact. They read books about women called Kimberley Delaware who get rushed off their feet by fellows called Lance Piston. They flock to Meryl Streep movies, and they read magazines filled with stories about love and fulfillment. They go out with totally unsuitable men and convince themselves they're in love. And what does it all lead to? Drapes. That's the point of it all. All that romance and heaving bosoms and high-octane passion. Drapes. All those meaningful glances, all those romantic dinners for two, all the heartfelt vows uttered between satin sheets. It all builds up to the most important walk a man and a woman make together: the walk into the drapery department. Every woman has dreamed of this moment, when she and her man shop for drapes.

Try romance then. Try touching her in those intimate places as you roam among the drapes, and see where it gets you. What does the expression "short shrift" mean to you? "Honestly, Roger, get your mind out of the gutter." The gutter? Is this the woman whose bosom once heaved at your very touch?

Where does it all go wrong? Social scientists have pinpointed a moment within 24 hours of a marriage proposal. That tender creature who professed an undying interest in your stories about sports and cars suddenly turns all business when it comes to the wedding invitations. Romance founders on the rocks of the guest list, and it sinks in the drapery department.

There are other funny things about women. Take fingernails. The only people who can be forgiven for becoming obsessed about their fingernails are classical guitarists and knuckleball pitchers. Yet there are women who devote hours a day to their nails, particularly to growing them as long as possible, thus making their hands useless for any normal tasks. A stiff breeze can damage a nail and ruin a day.

For whom are women growing these grotesque fingernails? Certainly not for men. A recent survey of men revealed a unanimous dislike of talons on women. And how about makeup in the Tammy Faye Bakker school of face-painting? Same thing.

Women get all this stuff from women's magazines. Men know all about men's magazines, but little about the female counterparts.

Unimaginative men might suppose that women's magazines feature lyrical photo features of scantily-clad men, making the same sort of ridiculous facial expressions that men are used to seeing in their own magazines. Not so, it turns out. In fact, the scantily-clad gentleman hardly appears at all in the women's mags. Remarkably enough, most women show little interest in pictorial displays of naked men. Studies done at random newsstands across the nation reveal that the women who buy *Playgirl*, for instance, are invariably buying it as a joke for a sick or depressed girlfriend.

No, interestingly enough, what you'll see a lot in women's magazines are photographs of scantily-clad women. This is one of the mysteries about women. Presumably in these ecology-conscious days, whole forests could be saved by combining men's and women's magazines. A photo feature on Lulubelle, 19, could well include her make-up tips, some of her favourite recipes, and a full description of the filmy garment she has abandoned at the side of the hot tub, not to mention hints on how to catch and keep a man.

This is another thing about women. Apparently a whole lot of them are desperate to find a man. They're considering just about anything to get one. Read the magazines. It's true. Which may come as a surprise to the men who are still being told to buzz off. But men should be careful. A closer examination of women's magazines will reveal what is behind this dedicated man hunt. Do not fool yourself. A woman may approach you in a bar, dazzle you with a pair of sparkling eyes (watch for tinted contacts), and make some of the most provocative suggestions you have ever heard outside your own fantasies. Keep a grip on your heart, and whatever else may be fluttering. This woman is after only one thing, and she's willing to do damn near anything to get it. She will step over anyone and anything to attain her ultimate goal. Yes, my friend, I'm talking drapes.

COPING WITH THE OPPOSITE SEX
'Personals' Columns Explained

Increasingly these days, people seeking companionship, sex, perversion, or even marriage, are turning to the personals columns of daily newspapers. They are a social and sexual smorgasbord, but to the uninitiated, they might as well be written in Swedish. Here then, is what is being said and what is meant. *Bon appetit.*

WM — white male
BF — black female
GWF — gay white female
W? — white person of uncertain gender
AC/DC — bisexual
ac/dc — electrician
dc/ac — bad electrician
ST — siamese twins
GST — gay siamese twins
Bi F — bisexual female
Buy F — female shopper
B'y F — female from Newfoundland
Baa F — female sheep

gdlkng — good looking
nsmkr — non-smoker
jdkwxpy — broken typewriter
'Macho' — one big eyebrow
'Feminist' — hairy legs
'Sensitive' — lives with mother
'Insensitive' — sleeps with mother
'Supersensitive' — sleeps with father
'Brawny' — fat athlete
'Cuddly' — fat non-athlete
'Well-rounded' — fat slob
'Pleasantly-plump' — fat
'Rubenesque' — fat lady
'statuesque' — tall fat lady
'complicated' — multiple personalities, all of them dull
'uncomplicated' — no personality
'no strings' –- wham, bam, thank you m'am
'strings' — bondage
'stallion' — goof with gold chains
'dude' — black goof with gold chains
'prude' — goof with rosary beads
'fun-loving' — slut
'free spirit' — slut with a car
'loves to laugh' — happy slut
'generous' — he pays
'practical' — seperate cheques
'momma's boy' — momma pays
'romantic' — cries at movies
'quiet' — socially retarded
'exotic' –- refugee
'mature' — wears dentures
'multi-faceted' — no steady job
'unconventional' — potential psychiatric patient
'zany' — current psychiatric patient
'wild 'n' crazy' — feral psychiatric patient

COPING
WITH GOD

God is not to be fooled with. God is omnipotent, omniscient, omnipresent, and omniverous. By comparison, the rest of us are ambiguous, ambivalent, and, at best, ambidextrous. We are not worthy to touch the hem of His garment, if in fact He wears a garment. If He does wear a garment, we can probably assume He designs it, makes it, and does His own dry-cleaning, for who else would be worthy? Perhaps He has created a sort of middle-level being, someone (probably a woman) who is worthy not only to touch the hem of His garment but also to wash and iron it. If so, He has not told the rest of us. Perhaps that is what happens to saints after a life of doing good down here. They get to cook and clean for Himself.

Does God eat? If it is true that He created us in His own image, as we are told, then He probably stuffs Himself as we do. Does He have to worry about cholesterol? Does He watch His weight? Does He look like Orson Welles by now? And — how can we express this — does he produce waste products, or is he like the British Royal Family?

And *which* image anyway? Does He look like Arnold Schwarzenegger, Kareem Abdul-Jabbar, and Woody Allen all at once? Does He take turns? Is He clean shaven? Does He have long hair like His son? Is He subject to fashion in these matters like the rest of us?

There are so many questions about God. Unfortunately, the *Bible* leaves most of them unanswered. What about the business of God being a guy? How do we know? Is it because the world is just the sort of place we can picture having been created by a man — messy, smelly, no closets, and some horrendous colour combinations? If He is a man, does He sometimes crave a little female company? Does He do anything about it? Is He gay? Look, I'm just asking.

More important, what motivates God? Put yourself in His shoes for a second. Say you've created the world. Picture it. You have singlehandedly — and in the space of a mere week — created a world that encompasses people and cacti and turtles and aardvarks and cockroaches and jellyfish and all the rest of it. Good job! You have displayed verve and imagination on a scale we can only wonder at. You have dazzled us with beauty. You have made things so tiny that nobody ever saw them until the invention of the microscope. Not to put too fine a point on it, you have blown our little minds.

Now, having created spiders' webs, rainbows, and the ingredients for draught Guinness, suddenly you turn petty and spiteful. Along come the rules. Having created sex, you turn around and create marriage. No sex beforehand. No messing about afterwards. No contraception. No doing it yourself. No doing it at all without the clear intention of making new people. Well, excuse me. How come animals don't have to get married?

Mind you, if you like rules, you're going to love the "Book of Deuteronomy." If you can read "Deuteronomy" with a clear conscience, you've lived a very dull life indeed. Chapter twenty-two, for instance, bars you from appearing in drag, and tells you how much it costs to lie with an unbetrothed virgin (fifty shekels of silver, and you have to marry her). The same chapter very arbitrarily forbids you from plowing with an ox and an ass together. As sins go, this one is fairly easy to resist, but one objects on principle. Immediately after that rule, you get "Thou shalt not wear a garment of divers sorts, as of woollen and linen together." Does that eliminate 50% cotton, 50% polyester?

You want unfair? Try this one on for size. Chapter twenty-three, verse one: "He that is wounded in the stones, or hath his privy member cut off, shall not enter into the congregation of the Lord." Say what? Does that mean what I think it means? Now, that's tough.

It goes on and on. Now skip to chapter twenty-eight. This one tells you what *happens* if you plow with an ox and an ass simultaneously, or wear that tacky shirt you got for Christmas. You'd better sit down. You're going to be cursed in the city and in the field, cursed when you come in and when you go out. The Lord's going to smite you with consumption, fever, inflammation, extreme burning, with the sword and with blasting and with mildew. Wait, it gets worse. The Lord's going to smite you with the botch of Egypt, the emerods, the scab, and the itch, with madness, blindness, and astonishment of heart. Another man will lie with your betrothed, your sons and daughters will go into captivity, locusts will eat your crops, and your ass will be violently taken from you. The book goes on to detail the sort of unpleasant foreigners who will come and invade you and eat all your food and besiege you and drive you to eat your own children, and you'll get all the diseases of Egypt and more besides. Finally, you'll be taken to Egypt itself and sold into slavery, except that nobody will ever buy you. Scarcely surprising, given that unsightly botch.

Most modern clergymen play down this rather hard-hitting look at God — well, it's hardly a sympathetic view, is it? — but the rules are still around. And nobody has rules like the Catholics. (How come all the lawyers are Jews? You'd think they'd be Catholics.) Yet God is forever changing the rules, even for Catholics. Not that long ago, He was adamant about Catholics saying mass in Latin and not eating meat on Fridays. What happened? God suddenly changed His mind? Price of fish go up? Was He the target of a lobbying blitz by the cattle-breeding interests? Did He discover that more kids were studying sex education than Latin? And how did He make the announcement? A word in the Pope's ear? "Oh, and by the way, about that fish on Friday business — tell them to forget it. Hey, did you notice I wasn't speaking in Latin?"

And He's waffled a bit about contraceptives over the years, too. As H.L. Mencken observed: "It is now quite lawful for a Catholic woman to avoid pregnancy by a resort to mathematics, though she is still forbidden to resort to physics and chemistry."

Shopping around for God? The Catholic God, as noted, has become a little mealymouthed in recent years, though He does have an impressive repertoire behind Him, what with the Inquisition and all. He has inspired some magnificent music in the past, but not much recently. He still does a nice line in guilt, particularly in conjunction with sex.

The Jewish God inspires a delightful kind of fatalism that has long been the mainstay of American humour. Until Bob Newhart, there had almost never been a funny American gentile. The food is good and filling, but the music, if you're not born to it, can be jarring.

The Protestant God takes many forms. The God of Oral Roberts, it seems to this observer, is not one to rush to, being a tawdry extortionist at heart. The "Rev." Ian Paisley's God, likewise, is a violent, intolerant sort of deity, and probably talks with an abrasive Ulster Protestant accent. Ernest Angley's cheerful God seems an improvement, but I'd avoid Jerry Falwell's slick, corporate Lord.

Frankly, most of the Protestant Gods are a trifle low on levity, and condemn drinkin' and dancin' and general carryin' on. Most of them also seem to be decidedly right wing. This critic's tip is the Anglican/Episcopalian God. Usually to be found in pleasing settings, the Anglican/Episcopalian God is low on theology, high on ambience and good music. He is easy-going on most of the sins, and enjoys a drop of decent sherry. Thus He tends to attract a better class of follower. Remember that the church was established by Henry VIII, a high-liver if ever there was one. Bishop Tutu's an Anglican, and he seems a pretty jolly fellow, with a hell of a cute name.

Really, who else is there? The Jehovah's Witnesses have gone up in the estimation of many of us since they booted Michael Jackson out, but all that door-to-door stuff is a real pain. And in any case, you're too late to be one of the hundred and forty-four thousand elect, so what's the point? The Christadelphians have a funny name, but is that enough? The Mormons? Have you ever been to Salt Lake City?

Then there's all those eastern religions, but the paperwork involved in changing your name is a drag, not to mention the embarrassment of trying to remember whether the Baba comes before the Rama or after. And that's without getting into the funny clothes. If you want to wear a uniform, join the Salvation Army. At least they'll let you eat meat.

The Moonies are fashionably right wing, but they'll try to tell you who to marry. The Bhagwan is out of business, and the Hari Krishna rhythm bands appear to have gone the way of Crosby, Stills, Nash, and Young.

Or you could always do without. You can catch most of it on TV. Maybe you're cynical enough that you don't need to go to church. Hell, Ron and Nancy don't, so why should you?

SEVEN MORE DEADLY SINS

Wrath, Pride, Lust, Avarice, Gluttony, Envy and Sloth; these are the Seven Deadly Sins, or that used to be the case back when things were simple. Today, life is a lot more complicated and the old stand-bys just don't cover the social crimes that are now found morally unacceptable. Seven more Deadly Sins have been added.

Malnetworking. Association, beyond a perfunctory level, with jerks, loose has-beens, and people from the mailroom.

Buckpassery. Overreliance on the phrase 'It's not my job . . . '

Patboonism. Being persistently and nauseatingly positive and upbeat.

Teleshirkery. Unwholesome urge to *not* leave your name and number and brief message at the sound of the tone.

Screwtoppity. The serving of cheap domestic wines to party guests later in the evening.

Fawnebbish. Slavish admiration of *everything* by Woody Allen.

Tarlickery. The persistent wearing of white shoes and belt by anyone under eighty.

TEN REASONS
TO STAY ALIVE
The Cynic's Guide To The Future

All right, no one's saying it's a lot of fun being alive. And nobody's going to blame you if you choose to exercise the extreme option. Suicide, after all, is the ultimate democratic act. Talk about voting with your feet. It's not something to rush into, however. It's not a decision to take lightly. It's a little more complicated than deciding between, say, the fusilli with snow peas and juniper berries in a licorice sauce and the stuffed squid fingers with sun-dried tomatoes and ground acorns on a bed of braised endive stems.

The compilers of this book are not about to discourage you from taking whatever rash act you feel these dreadful times call for, though we'd hate to lose a reader. It's something you have to decide for yourself. We would, however, implore you to consider the matter. Suicide is so final, don't you find? A bad dinner you can send back to the kitchen, but a suicide is forever.

After all, things could get better. It's statistically unlikely, we're the first to admit, but somebody's winning all those lotteries, unless they're really hiring actors to pose as happy winners for the newspapers. What keeps most of us from dispatching ourselves from this dreary world of lawyers, new diseases, in-laws, Sean Penn, TV evangelists, and the designated hitter rule is, when all is said and done, the niggling fear that we might miss something. Our enemies might be exposed and humiliated. The weather might improve. The Chicago Cubs might . . . well, there's a limit to this sort of thing.

Think of this: it is statistically probable that someone somewhere early in 1987 left a suicide note declaring that he couldn't go on living in a world in which Gary Hart was the Democrats' presidential front-runner. Wouldn't you feel silly now if that had been you?

Despite all the evidence, there are reasons to go on. The following is only a partial list of upcoming events that you would regret missing if you did yourself in.

January, 1989
Ronald Reagan leaves office. You may have won the office pool to guess how many polyps he has removed while in the White House.

August 6, 1990
Centenary of first use
of electric chair,
Auburn, NY.

Winter, 1991
Gary Hart announces
intention of running
for president.

Spring, 1991
Gary Hart withdraws
from race.

December, 1991
Celebrate the 100th
anniversary of the
invention of basketball
and the 50th anniversary
of Pearl Harbor. Think of
the party possibilities.

October, 1992
Five hundredth anniversary of Columbus's voyage to America. Watch for massive opportunities to celebrate by groups representing Vikings, Welsh, Irish, Phoenicians, and native Americans.

September, 1993
Gala celebrations of 75th anniverary of Boston Red Sox' last World Series championship.

February, 1998
One hundredth anniversary of the sinking of the battleship *Maine* in the Spanish-American War. Think of the fabulous commemorative stamp.

January 8, 2000
Elvis would have turned sixty-five.

Summer, 2062
Return of Halley's Comet. Well, it's got to be better than last time.

COPING WITH ADVERSITY

If It Wasn't For Bad Luck, I Wouldn't Have No Luck At All

Coping with adversity. Well, what else is there? Quick — what's the opposite of adversity? You can't think of it, can you? That's why you're a cynic. Serendipity, perhaps. When did you last experience serendipity? When's the last time you leaned back, smiling seraphically, absolutely carefree, and said to yourself (or someone else), "Now this is serendipity!"

No, adversity is our natural state. Sure, sometimes life is briefly "nice" or even "pleasant," but chances are your head will be pounding in the morning. That will be adversity. You will not be surprised when it hits you. You've seen it before.

Some of us handle adversity better than others. Mind you, some of us are paid better than others for handling adversity. But even rich people crack up in the face of it, which in the view of the rest of us is incredibly satisfying. With all due respect to rich people, the sight of the well-to-do going off the rails is one of the few edifying and thoroughly enjoyable forms of entertainment left to those of us whose lives comprise endless, squalid encounters with our creditors.

So, how to handle adversity? How to behave when life is even worse than usual? How to break through that nasty old cloud and get to that much-promised silver lining.?It's not easy, but let the compilers of *The Cynic's Guide* steer you right. You think the book game's a bed of roses? No sir-ee Bob! But we keep smiling through it all. Here are a few of our tips:

1. Visit cemetaries. You think you've got it bad? Look at all the suckers around you. Dead as doornails, every one of them. (If you begin to envy them, try another technique.)

2. Memorize Kiplings's hackneyed poem "If." Recite it sardonically and at great volume in inappropriate places, giving undue emphasis to the particularly cloying bits. To vary this technique, make up silly lines to insert wherever they fit. For example: "If you can keep your head while all about you/ Are losing theirs and blaming it on you/ You've probably misunderstood the problem/ Apologize and say you've got the 'flu."

3. Sing an obnoxiously cheerful song. If you are musically inclined, try singing it in a minor key. This is very effective with a song like "Bibbity-Bobbity-Boo." "Whistle a Happy Tune," from *The King and I* is another good one, and has the virtue of being the only clean song most of us can think of that includes the word "erect." Sing it with all new gusto. See how many parts of the body you can substitute for "head."

4. Sing an obnoxiously inspirational song. "Climb Every Mountain" is good, as are "The Long and Winding Road" and "Bridge Over Troubled Water." Try singing them with different foreign accents. Guaranteed to provoke a smile. Classical buffs might enjoy whistling bits from great requiems. Imagine the "Pié Jésu" from Faure's *Requiem* performed by an amateur Dixieland band.

5. See how many of the Watergate felons you can recall. Remember the song Danny Kaye used to sing made up of the names of Russian composers? Try doing the same with the Watergate boys. Try them to the tune of *Yesterday*:

Erlichman
Colson, Kalmbach, Dean, and Haldeman,
Mitchell, Liddy, Hunt, and Fred Larue,
Magruder, Krogh, Dwight Chapin too.

See if you can get the whole bunch into one song. Don't forget
Eugenio Martinez and Frank Sturgis.

6. Make anagrams of the names of great people of our times. With
pratice you'll be able to turn Spiro Agnew into Grow A Penis, or
Ronald Reagan into A Real Drag, Non?

7. Make a list of everybody you've ever seen naked, and rate them
from zero to ten. Leave photocopies of the list where people will
see it.

8. Put your right hand under your left armpit and make farting noises.

9. Play music by slapping your hands against your face while opening
and closing your mouth.

10. Fake your death by leaving your clothes and identification in a
pile on a beach, then start a new life in Brazil.

COPING WITH SOCIETY'S PROBLEMS
Knowing Where to Place the Blame

Since the dawn of man, the easiest way of coping with society's problems has been to blame them on somebody else. *'Scapemastadons'* these were known as. Later they became 'scapegoats.' Visible minorities have always been a favorite choice. The Goths blamed the Visigoths, the Romans blamed the Christians, the French blamed the bourgeoisie.

It's high time we deregulated the scapegoat industry; brake free of the old stand-bys and strictures and strike out in bold new directions of blame-laying. It's easy, for example, to blame your troubles on "radical, spam-licking Rotarians." Make up your own, or simply choose one word each from columns A, B, and C.

A	B	C
goddam	tofu-crazed	Belgians
frigid	four-eyed	polyglots
#@*&+ !	button-downed	marsupials
bloated	cheese-eating	Munchkins
bloodsucking	bush-league	Hottentots
backstabbing	short-sighted	ecclesiasts
%¢*##@ !	bleeding-heart	neo-ignoroids
smirking	snot-nosed	thespians
flatulent	A-cup	post-impressionists
godless	knuckle-cracking	spelunkers
Satanic	glue-sniffing	Alsace-Lorrainians
pseudo	non-designer	flautists
hedonistic	acid-tongued	bi-valves
subsidized	half-assed	aviatrixes
gibbering	non-conformist	column C creeps

THE SNIDES

HOW TO MAKE FRIENDS AND USE PEOPLE

It's a dog-eat-dog world. Every cynic knows that and acknowledges that this accounts for the appearance of numerous bestselling dog-training manuals and other "How To" books. As a true cynic, you have avoided buying any book in the "How To" genre, but you also suspect that the authors of these books just might know something that you don't.

Well, here is the definitive guide, written exclusively with the cynic in mind, that will teach you how to meet people and use them according to your needs and the dictates of your social calendar.

We all remember *How to Make Friends and Influence People.* But why bother expending all that energy to impress and be impressed. After all, you don't want to befriend everyone, you only want to *seem* to befriend them just in case you need their services or support.

Every cynic should have a large circle of acquaintances and each of the following professionals should be represented:

GROUP A

lawyer	doctor
psychoanalyst	orthodontist
accountant	plastic surgeon
stock broker	colour consultant
	hair stylist

If these professionals are not represented, you should make every effort to get to know one, just in case it becomes necessary to ask for their services for free as "a close personal friend" or at least get very cut rates.

A novel approach to introduce and endear yourself to a useful professional is to enlist the help of your children. For example, the parent of your child's classmate is targeted for your A list. Have *your* child befriend *their* child and invite him for an overnight. Give the kid the time of his life. After all, his idea of a terrific time is a lot cheaper than entertaining his parents at a four-star restaurant. The child will return home to his parents, extolling your qualities as a parent and praising your generosity. These stories will make the child's parents feel indebted to you. If they attempt to reciprocate by inviting your child over, politely decline, explaining that, unfortunately, your entire family is spending the weekend in the Seychelles, and, although you would love to be able to invite their son along, unfortunately your private jet only seats six. Unable to reciprocate, they remain in your debt. By the time they finally meet you, at a parent/teachers night, they will be so intrigued by your lifestyle that they will invite you to dinner at their home. Remain aloof and distant while you drop hints about your life. They'll be hooked and ready to serve at your beck and call.

If this tried and true method is not your style of *modus operandi*, you might consider using the barter system — a system whereby you connect the needy parties from your A list with people from your B list.

GROUP B

plumber	beautician
electrician	BMW mechanic

| aerobics instructor | performance artist |
| contract killer | pool maintenance person |

As middleperson, you connect the parties, the needed with the needy. For example, a lawyer requires the services of a plumber, a portly stockbroker needs a private aerobics instructor, and your colour consultant is in desperate need of a hit man. In lieu of a fee, just keep score of your markers, until it becomes necessary for you to call them in.

But having the necessary contacts to obtain the services of professionals and tradespeople for free doesn't always fulfill your needs for all occasions. For instance, you are throwing a party for your spouse. The party will also serve as a way to impress the top pros on your A list, who will no doubt be impressed by the sheer number of "close personal friends" who attend. But who would want to bother with actually maintaining that many friendships It is much better to cultivate Group C — incorporating a group of characters that wish to make contact with the people of your A and B lists.

GROUP C

performance artist	sex therapist
acupuncturist	comedy writer
hypnotherapist	experimental filmmaker

Finally, should the need arise, it is wise to keep a tentative list of candidates for Group D — people who can be contacted and, at a moment's notice, pad the guest list at functions such as weddings, bar mitzvahs, funerals, and your child's first piano recital.

POSSIBLE CANDIDATES FOR GROUP D

| The Black Watch Pipers | a local NHL franchise |
| the original cast of *Hair* | The Mormon Tabernacle Choir |

Yes, it's easy to make friends and use people, just remember this simple rule; always take them before they can take you.

HOW CELEBRITIES COPE

"I do it myyyyyyyyyyyy way." *Frank Sinatra*

"I limp and I lie." *Richard M. Nixon*

"I roll my eyes and hunch my shoulders and kind of loll my head all around." *Stevie Wonder*

"Me too." *Ray Charles*

"I content myself in the knowledge that a 76-year-old heart has only so many more beats in it." *George Bush*

"I take short naps. I can drop off just anyw . . . . . " *Ronald Reagan*

"I don't leave home without it" (American Express card) *Karl Malden*

"I don't leave home without it" (.38 calibre handgun) *Bernard Goetz*

"We always get our man." *The RCMP*

"So do I." *Joan Collins*

"And we always get the pictures." *National Enquirer*

From the Desk of
𝕯𝖗. 𝕽𝖚𝖙 𝖁𝖊𝖘𝖙𝖍𝖆𝖒𝖒𝖊𝖗

Hello zere!

I'm Dr. Rut. How are you zis morning? Good. Zat's nice. Und quite normal too. Zose erections in ze morning are a *perfectly normal physical phenomenon* — and ze ladies best friend — if you'll excuse Dr. Rut for making ze little joke, ha, ha!

But zeriously, ve are currently zeeing ze great changes in ze sex business, like vot haf never been zeen before, und Dr. Rut has zeen it all!

It's zis AIDZ; Aquired Immune Diviciency Zyndrome. It's ze beggest pain in ze patootie zince ze yeast invection. Rigor mortis iz no zubztitute for ze natural erection. People is scared. Zere taking ze precautions. Zos condoms! Talk about taking ze shower in ze raincoat! Zere recommending abstinance. Are zey kiddin? Even vith 129 channels, ze cable TV iz no subztitute. Monogamy? All vell und good, for a veek or two, but vhat zen?

Vell you've just got to cope. Guidelines can help vith zis. Even ze game of 'Hide Ze Salami' has to have ze rules ha, ha!

Yours in ze copulation,

Dr. Rut

Dr. Rut Vesthammer is the world's foremost authority on sex. Contrary to widespread public opinion, however, she did not invent sex, although she was instrumental in perfecting it in the labs and motels of post-war Germany.

Dr. Rut is married and achieves simultaneous orgasm every time.

DR. RUT RULES
FOR COPING WITH
MODERN SEXUALITY

1. Say 'Is it in yet?' only in cases of extreme uncertainty.

2. Claim virginity only in the presence of three wise men bearing gifts.

3. Ensure your partners comfort; no 'Mohawk' styles for pubic hair.

4. Demand details of your partner's past sexual history, and call for confirmation.

5. 'Love handles' are acceptable, but not if you can balance a beer on them.

6. Loss of erection three times in a row means you're gay.

7. Avoid phrases like 'stretch marks,' 'pencil-dick,' and 'I want my money back.'

8. Mr. Right never is.

9. Anyone with 'Property of the Hells Angels' tatooed on their buttocks does not want to meet your parents.

10. Oysters are aphrodisiacs only to other oysters.

COPING WITH TRAVEL

*A man travels the world over in search of what he needs
and returns home to find it.*
George Moore

Which is surely a roundabout way of saying that there's no place like home for the holidays. Still, people will travel, and it is scarcely the purpose of this book to discourage them. Go out there and see the world, by all means. Just remember: there are 5 billion people in the world today, of which more than 95% are foreigners. If you travel to other countries, you will almost certainly meet some of them.

It is important to take great care in dealing with foreigners. They will try to cheat you and rob you. At the very least they will attempt to embarrass you. It is their nature, and there is no point trying to change them. They simply haven't had our advantages. You only have to look at their bathrooms to see this. To be blunt — the squeamish should stay at home.

Still, most of us will be tricked by unscrupulous travel agents into going to foreign countries at some time in our lives. The point is not to travel like a wimp. Don't let them beat you. Travel like an American. Here are some rules to protect you.

RULE ONE

Be assertive. Foreigners delight in announcing that certain products are not available right now or that certain services cannot be offered. They are simply being lazy. Be strict with them. There is no reason you should have to settle for less than you would expect at home. You're paying a bundle to be in their crummy country; demand the best. If the truth be known, they will respect you for it.

Say, for instance, you are in Scotland in July. The temperature is barely above freezing, and your hotel is unheated. You ask politely for heat, only to be told that the central heating is turned off because it's the middle of the summer. Raise hell. Tell the hotel keeper that you'd get heat at a Travelodge *and* pay a damn sight less for the privilege.

At this point, your man will try to snow you by speaking in his quaint Scottish dialect. "Och," the cringing wretch will say, "I dinna ken yer Travelodge, but . . . ." This is the moment of truth. Many innocent tourists fall into the trap. They meekly return to their ice-bound rooms, saying to each other, "What'd the old guy say?"
"I don't know, but it sure sounded cute as hell."
"Are we getting any heat?"
"Your guess is as good as mine, honey. Think he'd mind if I took his picture?"

Which brings us to another important point.

RULE TWO

Pretend you don't speak any foreign languages. We cannot stress this point enough. Never place a foreigner in a position in which he has the advantage. Make him speak your language. Don't worry — they *all* speak English. They might pretend otherwise, but don't you believe them. If you speak slowly enough and loudly enough, they'll understand all right. If your English is too sophisticated for them, they will appreciate it if you try a sort of childish pidgin-English. A request for a daily newspaper, for instance, would be "Me want *International Herald Tribune*." This seldom fails. (Incidentally, ignore the local papers, even if you can read them. They are filled with local nonsense and contain no baseball scores.)

RULE THREE

Next is some sound advice about currency. Americans abroad are often confused by local money. One day it's marks, the next day it's francs, and it may well be kroner the day after tomorrow. How do we keep track, people want to know. How do we know we're not getting ripped off? Our advice, plain and simple, is to ignore foreign money. It looks ridiculous, comes in funny shapes and colours, and is never worth the same for two days in a row. Ignore it. Carry nothing but the money you're used to — American greenbacks!

How many pfennigs in a deutschmark? Who cares? What's a drachma worth? Don't ask me! What's the correct change from a million-lira note when you buy a pack of Camels? The Italians know, but they sure as hell ain't going to tell you! Listen — *you* know what a pack of Camels cost. So pay the man! If he gives you a hard time, remind him who won the war. He'll back down in a hurry. Relax, everybody loves American dollars. It's international money, and you always know where you stand. Peel off a wad of greenbacks and the world's on your side.

RULE FOUR

Watch what you eat. You can get a hamburger of some sort in every reasonably-sized town in the western world. Ask for it well done, as some countries delight in raw food. Raw fish, raw meat, you name it. Just don't eat it. The French, as we all know, eat frogs' legs. To be safe, avoid French food altogether. Take canned goods with you. Don't drink the water anywhere.

RULE FIVE

Stick up for yourself. Remember that the foreigner is going to try something. So do it to him before he does it to you. Remind people constantly about the war. Particularly in Germany or Japan. (Actually, you're best to avoid Japan altogether. Raw fish *and* a huge trade surplus. And they're notoriously inscrutable. You can bring up Hiroshima but they won't rise to the bait, though you can sometimes get their goat by scrunching your face up and saying "Rotsa ruck!" But you'll still pay $200 a night for your hotel.)

Even our allies take well to reminders of the war. After all, they sure were glad to have us on their side way back then. And they're still grateful to Americans to this day. One wrong look from a Frenchman, for instance, and you can fire off a quick "Look buster, if it weren't for us you'd be speaking Kraut today!" It works like a charm. Walk into an English pub and say "Anybody here remember General Eisenhower?" You won't have to pay for a drink, you can count on that.

RULE SIX

Americans are well-loved around the globe, so take advantage of it and let 'em know where you're from. Otherwise they might think you're just a Canadian or something. Wear distinctive clothing. Everybody the world over recognizes a stetson. So what if you're from Vermont! Loud checked pants and contrasting jacket make a fashion statement that tells the world you know who you are. Go for it!

Having said that, it must be noted that there are a few soreheads out there with a barrelful of chips on their shoulders where we're concerned. We're talking about terrorists here, folks, and they're no joke. These are guys who never worked a day in their lives, expect a free ride, and blame everything on the Americans. *The Herald Tribune* will let you know when the terrorism count is high, and when it is advisable to change your game-plan. Wear more sedate clothing. Leave your stetson at the hotel. Wear a maple leaf pin in your lapel. That's right, friends — pretend you're Canadian. You can get easy-to-apply, easy-to-remove Canadian-flag decals for your luggage. Talk about snow. Be self-effacing. Smart Americans have been doing the fake Canadian routine for years now, ever since this terrorism business got going. Observers noted that in the treacherous summer of 1986 — the summer of Mad-Dog Khadafi — an estimated 25,000,000 Canadians visited Europe. That's every man, woman, and child in Canada.

RULE SEVEN

As an American, you like to call people by name. This can be difficult in foreign countries, where the locals invariably have stupid foreign names that are tough to pronounce. And if you start to laugh while saying Wolfgang or Bjorn or some damn fool name, some foreigners may take offence. They're like that. Avoid the problem by avoiding names. Don't even listen when they tell you their names. It will only tempt you to try saying them, especially if you've had a schnapps or two. Female foreigners always answer to Sweetheart or Honey, while male foreigners can be called Bud, Buster, or Pal.

RULE EIGHT

If you can't handle rules one through seven, then stick to rule eight. Ignore the rest of the world altogether and stay home this year. Go to Disneyworld or the Grand Canyon. Drive your own car on your own side of the road. In America, when you meet foreigners, you can treat them like foreigners. See America first, where toilets are terrific and you understand the sports' rules. And where people just like you will look you in the eye and say, "Have a nice day!"

COPING WITH DEJA VU
Why The Eighties
Are Like The Fifties

Well, all right, so Bruce Springsteen hasn't been drafted and sent to Germany. None of these analogies ever works out exactly right. Not even the Fifty-Two Uncanny Similarities Between Kennedy and Lincoln. But face it — if Reagan were a golfer instead of a napper, things would be just about the same.

Look at popular culture, if you can stand it. Prince and Michael Jackson even look a bit like Little Richard, only not as butch. Sean Penn gets arrested as often as Jerry Lee Lewis and Chuck Berry, albeit for less interesting crimes. Madonna's like Gogi Grant without the talent, and Elton John gets more like Liberace every day. What's the "Bill Cosby Show" if not a black "Leave it to Beaver?" And Cyndi Lauper? Gidget with the wrong medication, that's all. We could go on and on. Try it yourself! See who can come up with the best comparison. Bob Dylan and Frankie Lane! Boy George and Johnnie Ray! It's fun for the whole family!

Political life hasn't changed much. We're still bickering with the Russians. Once again it's an American war hero doing battle with a stocky, balding, suddenly accessible Russian premier. (All right,

Reagan's not a war hero, but he thinks he is, which is probably worse.) We've got spies again. South and North Korea are squabbling. We've got congressional hearings in which prominent Americans quarrel over which of them is the most patriotic. (The McCarthy types may win this time.) Richard Nixon is even treated with respect again!

And look at us. Greed is back in. Home ownership is back in. Blacks and whites don't like each other any more; it's just like the Fifties. People don't have sex any more, or if they do they use condoms. Kids are getting careers again. People under thirty are buying life insurance. The Top Forty is back. Jesus is back on the front page. Gadgets and labour-saving devices are back. Reagan's got us feeling good about ourselves again. Hell, maybe Detroit will give us fins again. Let's guzzle that gas!

You're right. It's depressing. You hated the Fifties the first time. You remember the stupid clothes, the ugly furniture, and the miniature marshmallows. People talk about the music, but all you can remember are "Purple People Eater" and "Itsy-Bitsy Teeny-Weeny Yellow Polka Dot Bikini" and David Seville and the blasted Chipmunks. But cheer up. Look what happened to the Fifties. They ended! And you know what came next. Fun. Sex. Drugs.

It could happen again. There are signs. Look on the bright side: we've already discredited TV evangelists.

COPING WITH
THE RICH

The best way to cope with rich people is by being one. But if one can't *be* rich, the next best thing is to wish them ill. They have so much while most of us have so little; it's difficult not to indulge in a little malicious jealousy. After all, its both entertaining and free. In fact, next to copulating and pirating videos, it is one of the masses remaining few enjoyable pastimes.

To those coping with their lack of lucre by wishing misfortune on the moneyed, take solace in the following facts.

CAR PHONES CAUSE CANCER!

POLO PONIES ARE MORE VICIOUS AND UNPREDICATABLE THAN PIT BULLS!

PEOPLE WHO BOWL LIVE LONGER!

PRIVATE JETS ARE EIGHT TIMES MORE LIKELY TO EXPLODE ON IMPACT!

CANNIBAL NANNIES ON THE RISE!

* Source; The National Enquirer Institute for Pseudo — Scientific Research / Headline Division

I.Q. Schrapnel
President

NReh?

Greetings!

Hello neighbors and gun lovers on both sides of the border. As first president of the Canadian NReh? I'd like to thank our brothers in arms in the National Rifle Association for their support, encouragement, and shipments of second-hand handguns.

Canada's history is shorter and not nearly so violent as that of the United States, but with a little effort and your prayers, we can change all that.

We have a long way to go. Up here the term 'Saturday Night Special' means the latest Wayne and Shuster Comedy Hour on CBC. The only thing we've got a constitutional right to bear is regional resentment.

What Canada needs is a coast-to-coast network of ghetto pawnshops offering a large selection of cheap handguns. Our Conservative government, with their cutbacks in funding of social services, housing, and education, and consistantly unenlightened immigration policies, have done their bit in ghetto creation. More must be done. We continue to press the government to relax the regulations governing convenience stores. They are currently renting videos, processing film, and selling hot soups and sandwiches; can handguns be far behind? We hope not.

I must address the issue of Canada's chronic shortage of psychopaths. In America, deranged war veterens are a minor-league from which a proud tradition of serial killers, rooftop snipers, and supermarket-spree gunmen spring. Canada has no such natural resource. We must make do with cabin fever cases, glue sniffers and Brador drinkers. When Castro emptied his prisons and asylums,

and sent them, armed, to North America, a golden opportun-
ity to redress the imbalance was lost. Miami hogged
them all and all we get is the occasional Rastafarian.

There does seem to be one hopeful trend, that of
Canada's gallant shoot first, ask questions later all-
night pharmacists. The score thus far is Pharmacists 4-
Street Scum 0. So much excitement was caused by this that
it is rumored that a film production crew were scouting
locations in Saskatchewan for a new Charles Bronson film,
' Death Wish Pharmacist. *

I can report that our national game, ice hockey
has thus far resisted our lobbyists in arming players,
but a trial program of arming referees in Northern Ontario
mining community leagues has almost entirely eliminated
bench-clearing brawls.

I hesitate to end with a threat, but Hey, America!,
how come you're shipping arms to Iranians, who burn your
flag and call you 'The Great Satan', while good ol'
Canada gets the short end of the stick? Don't we take all
the acid rain and 'brewed under licence' Bud and Miller
Lite you can send us without complaint? Is hostage-taking
the only way to get your attention?

Well listen up! It is well known that most good
'American' comedy of the last decade is produced by
Canadians. SCTV, Saturday Night Live, National Lampoon...
all Canadian. Do you want it to continue, or do you want
to fall back on Henny Youngman and the Borscht Belt?
Send arms; good unregistered handguns; pieces, roscoes,
heaters, if you ever want to see your comedy alive again.
And tell ya what, just to show we're good sports, we'll
kick in a little to fund the Contras. Whaddaya say?

Yours, Armed to the teeth,

I. Q. Schrapnel,
President.

COPING WITH POPULAR MUSIC
Separating Myth From Reality

Okay, so to begin with, I guess everbody knows Jim Morrison isn't really dead, okay? Like, that's a given. I mean, about ten million people have seen his grave in Paris and got all choked up. But this guy is not in that grave, all right? Believe me. There's no question about this. The man lives to this day. I'm not entirely sure where he is, all right? I mean, he could be anywhere. But, like, he faked his death.

Well, look at it logically. He'd gone as far as he was going to go in rock music for that time, you understand? He was huge, I'm not kidding. I mean, he could not walk down the street. And also the cops were down on him with like more charges than you could imagine, you know, there was that indecent exposure bust and all the rest of it. And he was a poet, right? The man was a poet. And how can you be a poet if you can't even walk down the street, you dig? So like suddenly he's dead. In like mysterious circumstances. No questions asked. The man is dead at the age of twenty-eight. For no good reason, right?

So, I'm telling you, the man is alive. He's living somewhere in Europe writing poetry. Guy I know has talked to him in a bar in Dusseldorf. This is eight or nine years ago, so I don't know where he is now. The man is keeping a low profile on account of Interpol's after him over something we know nothing about. But the time will come when Jim's going to reappear, so we got to be ready for that day, man.

Now Bob Dylan's just the opposite. Bobby died in that motor-cycle crash back in the early seventies, only by that time he was so big for the record company that they hushed it up, paid some people off. This is true, man. Then they hired some guy who looked like Dylan, gave him two or three years to get his act together, then they sent him on the road. I mean, if you look at this dude up close you can see the difference. Look, you only have to listen to the songs, man. How many great songs has he done since the crash? Zero, man. Zilch.

Hey, figure it out. Ramblin' Jack Elliott goes to Dylan's place in Woodstock when he's supposedly recuperating from the crash, and Dylan won't even let the guy in the door. Same with Joan Baez, man. Like two of his closest friends he suddenly won't even see. And why's that? Because they're going to realize that the new Dylan's a fake, man. Think about it. Dylan's wife took the cash and didn't spill the beans, but she didn't stay married to the man, right? On account of it's a different guy! Face it, the old Bob Dylan wouldn't have done all this religious shit. Like born-again one week, then Jewish the next week. This new guy's in over his head. Guy I know was real tight with Dylan, he tells me the new guy's not even close.

Listen, don't even talk to me about Little Eva, man. There never was a Little Eva. Check this out. Play that record sometime, "Come on baby, do the locomotion with me." Then play your *Tapestry* album. Same voice, right? No question. Especially if you play the flip side to "Locomotion." You tell me that's not Carole King singing.

Hey, you've got to remember how the music biz worked in those days. You had a hit record, you went out on the road, did a year of one-night stands all over Idaho or some damn place. The money all went to the writers and producers, man. Look at Phil Spector. He did all the creative stuff, then sent these chick groups out on the road. You think they made any money?

Okay, I'm getting to it. So Carole King and Gerry Goffin write this song, "Come on baby do the locomotion with me," right? So you didn't have singer/songwriters in those days. You wrote the song, you hired some black kid to sing it. So, I don't know, maybe all the black kids were working somewhere else that day or something, but Carole King sings her own song in the studio. But does she want to tour Wisconsin for six months? No way. So they invent this Little Eva chick, make up this story like she's their babysitter, and send her out to lip-sync the song for the kids and sell some records. You think I'm making this up? Just listen to the song, man, that's all I'm saying.

Listen, everybody knows Ringo never played drums on any of the Beatles' records. This is fact, man. They hired studio guys to do it, then threatened them with violence if they talked. Well, the Mafia was behind the Beatles from the start. No, Paul wasn't dead, man. He just sounds like it. But the Mafia killed John. You didn't know that? Jeez, you surprise me. Sure, he had threatened to blow the whistle. He was too independent for their liking. It was a classic Mafia job, man. The guy steps out of his car, and boom.

No, it was the CIA that got Hendrix. He knew too much. There was a lot of heavy shit that was going down then. A drug overdose is real easy to fake, especially if you're the CIA. No — where the hell are you from, anyway? You think that Marvin Gaye was shot by his father? That's sure as hell what they want you to think. Hey, it's a hell of a lot more complicated than that. Marvin was tied in heavily with the Symbionese Liberation Army. He went to high school with Cinque, the dude that grabbed Patty Hearst. Marvin and Cinque went way back together. So when Cinque and the rest of them got offed in L.A., a lot of people thought that was the end of it. But there were some unanswered questions. And a few years later, boom — Marvin gets offed at short range by his father. Does that ring true to you, man?

Well draw your own conclusions. Dennis Wilson knows Charles Manson and he mysteriously drowns. A Beach Boy drowns? Get Away! And don't get me started on Janis, man. Hey, I guess you know it was a ham sandwich that got Mama Cass, eh? Well, I mean this is someone who was no stranger to a ham sandwich. You ever see her? And suddenly she's dead. It doesn't figure. Buddy Holly? Did I hear you say Buddy Holly? Listen, it's an open secret that there were a hell of a lot of drugs at Woodstock, guy I know was there and he told me . . . oh, and I guess you knew Grace Jones used to be a guy . . . .

COPING WITH
THE FUTURE

Every year it seems we have to cope with a new, improved, 'Scourge of Mankind.' Be they man-made, Act of God, or apocalyptic new disease, they appear without warning, and as regularly as Jerry Lewis telethons. Remember . . . .

1977 Killer bees
1978 Ford Pintos
1979 Hong Kong Flu
1980 Legionnaire's Disease
1981 Swine Flu
1982 Herpes II
1983 Iranian students
1984 AIDS
1985 Lybian terrorists
1986 Alzheimer's Disease
1987 Pit Bulls

Sparing no expense, *Cynic's Guide* has assembled an elite panel of psychics, seers, sooth-sayers, and charlatans from the cream of the supermarket tabloids. They have put their crystal balls together, and reveal here, exclusively for *Cynics Guide,* the catastrophes the next decade holds in store. Coping with them is *your* problem, but, as they say, *forewarned is forearmed.*

CYNIC'S GUIDE PSYCHICS PANEL

'Kourbassa'

Oscar

Mabel Leaf

J. Swifts

EXCLUSIVE *Cynic's Guide* predictions

1989: CANADIAN FLU A virulent strain of influenza with attendant symptoms of inferiority, indecisiveness, and a propensity to say "eh" will afflict millions of Americans during the winter of '89-'90. Oddly, a beneficial side-affect will be the dramatic increase in attendance at professional hockey games.

1991: NIPPON NISSAN SYNDROME Micro-organisms breeding in the windshield-washer fluids of Japanese import automobiles will trigger a North American epidemic of what will become known as NNS. The Japanese import market will become defunct overnight and North American automakers will accordingly double their prices.

1994: EMMANUEL LEWIS SYNDROME An inordinate number of multi-talented, black, dwarf babies born in the middle eighties will mature to find a dramatic shortage of television sit-coms to accomodate them. The disenfranchised and disenchanted youths will roam the inner cities in vicious, tapdancing gangs.

1996: SCALP CANCER The year 1996 will see a dramatic increase in the incidence of cancer of the scalp among women. This will be attributed to their annoying habit of wearing sunglasses atop their head.

1997: PLAGUES OF LOCUSTS, FROGS, FIREBALLS, ETC. Not seen since Biblical days, 'Rath of God' plagues will make a big comeback this year at the behest of television evangelists peeved about dwindling revenues.

COPING WITH GETTING OLDER

This section is designed for the older reader, one who has survived at least into their mid-thirties, one who has perhaps even ventured across the mystical barrier of 40. Now how bad was it? Hardly hurt a bit, am I right? You're still getting around not too badly, and once or twice a week you can stay up after 11 p.m. without being a total zombie next day.

You're doing fine. You can read this page without holding the book at arm's length or pressing your nose against the paper. And you don't look so bad either, let me tell you. Remember what 40-year-olds used to look like. Ancient, right? Back in the sixties, you used to vow you'd kill yourself rather than get like that. You wouldn't trust anyone over 30, so 40 was beyond the pale. Forty was the living dead.

But, hey, you look pretty good to me. Have you noticed that quite a few 40-year-olds don't look so bad these days? Seriously, could you ever have imagined yourself taking a second look at a 40-year-old? But it happens, doesn't it? You tell me.

Okay, granted, old age has its drawbacks. You get winded faster than you used to. Your dentist has uttered the dreadful word "periodontist." Your waistline isn't what it was. People your age are already washed up in fields like rock music and sports. If you were born before April 16, 1947, you are older than anyone playing in the NBA, the NFL, or the NHL. Baseball's a far more interesting and intelligent game anyway, and there are still some spry old birds playing in the big leagues. Even rock music has a few old fossils kicking about.

Yes, I know, you'd like to be 20 again. You had more fun when you were 20. You were getting stoned, getting laid, and getting back, or was it down? But were you really? Weren't you depressed a lot of that time? Hadn't you absorbed just enough existentialism to know that life was really pretty awful? That was when you were just showing the first signs of becoming a cynic. The difference is that a 40-year-old cynic can be remarkably cheerful about it all. The 20-year-old cynic gets depressed.

What did we have to get depressed about? Beer cost 15 cents a glass, pot was $15 an ounce, and love was free! But it was fashionable to get depressed. Some Fashion.

Okay, so maybe a genie offers you a free wish. Be careful how you word your answer. Don't just say, "I wish it were 1967 again." 'Cause you know what that old genie's going to do, don't you? He's going to make it 1967 again all right, but you're still going to be 40. Nobody's going to trust you, you're going to be fat and wrinkled, and you're going to stand out something fierce at those Jefferson Airplane concerts. You'll probably get tired and go home before the end. You looked silly in beads the first time around; you'll look bloody stupid now.

There is one worse possibility. You're going to look that genie in the eye and say, "I want to be 20 again!" And you will be. You'll be young and thin again. And it will be 1987. You think it's bad being 40 in the eighties? You ought to try being 20. Imagine thinking Madonna is somebody with talent. Imagine making an effort to get a ticket for a Level 42 concert. Imagine wanting to be as articulate and witty as the Beastie Boys.

Imagine having to talk loud all the time to try to impress your peers. Imagine knowing that if you go to the beach you'll get skin cancer because of the ozone or some damn thing. And you can't go skinny dipping anyway because there's nowhere secluded left, and the water's polluted, and it's not cool in any case these days. And if you tried to start a protest march, people your own age would tell you to get a job! But you can't get a good job because all those ex-hippie baby boomers twenty years older than you have them all wrapped up.

And then there's sex. When you were 20, you were laughing. The worst thing that was likely to happen was that you'd catch a few crabs. You had contraception and penicillin. Nowadays, if the pill or whatever doesn't kill you, the sex will. It used to be you worried that your bed partner might lay a guilt trip on you. Nowadays that person just might finish you off. The generation before yours sang "You always hurt the one you love," but this is getting ridiculous.

So relax. You have better taste in food and drink than you used to, and chances are you can even occasionally afford to indulge it. If you can't tell U2 from UB40, who cares? So what if you haven't been able to make out a pop music lyric since 1974? They're not talking to you anyway. And they're such wimps these days that they're not even singing about how stupid you are, the way we used to sing about our elders. So go on doing what you're doing. Play your Grateful Dead albums from time to time, and go on recycling your bottles and newspapers, even if the young people laugh at you. Do try to put a little bit aside for your old age, so you won't have to depend on the next generation. If the genie offers you that wish, use it to pay off the mortgage. With any luck, by the time today's 20-year-olds screw up the world, we'll all be dead.

COPING WITH THE LANGUAGE OF BUSINESS

Sorry, but it isn't possible to cope with the language of business. Just try to keep a straight face, dress conservatively, play squash, and read newspapers without pin-up girls.

THE TROUBLE WITH SPORTS
Take Me Out of the Ballgame

The modern sports scene in North America holds plenty of scope for the cynic. All the games we play are getting consistently worse, yet more and more people are willing to spend more and more money to go and watch them. We are living in an era in which a strike-out prone outfielder threatens to leave baseball forever if his team doesn't let him play pro football in his spare time, as a "hobby." This is an age in which there are more world boxing champions than ever before. Quick: name any of the current world middleweight champions. No, I couldn't either.

This is also a time in which Americans have trouble competing. According to the computer, the best golfers in the world are, in order, Australian, German, and Spanish. The leading American golfer is recognizable only by his funny trousers. Even in women's golf, things are getting out of hand. A Japanese player has been scary on the women's tour lately, and two different English women won the U.S. and British women's Open in successive weeks. The only top-ranked American tennis player is a woman who speaks with a Czech accent, and she's in the process of being surpassed by a German teenager. The fastest runner in the world is Canadian, the best decathlete is

British. American marathoners are also-rans, and the World Cup, Formula One Championship, and the Tour de France all go on without much showing from the *Stars and Stripes*.

Fortunately, Americans play a couple of games that few other people play. Americans always win the World Series, for example, though they refuse to play the Cubans. And on a *per capita* basis the Dominican Republic must also be something of a threat. And the Russians have covertly taken up the game in apparent preparation for the 1992 Olympics, so watch out. So far not many countries have taken up American football, probably because other countries hold their youth in higher esteem than to send them out to butt heads with each other. But even that's beginning to change, so America is not safe.

There are, of course, more Americans playing hockey than ever before, but it's still by and large the bailiwick of a bunch of toothless guys from Canada, which explains why most Americans have resisted taking to the game. You don't see it on network TV, for instance, do you? Sure the boys in the red, white, and blue beat the Rooshkies once, but it hasn't happened since. There may have been something funny in the Lake Placid water that week.

Luckily American baseball players don't have to play anyone else. Even the Canadian teams are nothing but Americans and Latins. So baseball's doing just fine. Sure, it's thick with lawsuits, and one of the game's most respected executives said on national television that blacks aren't smart enough to hold down responsible jobs, but ticket sales are doing just fine, thank you. So what if it takes three hours these days to play even a low-scoring game? Better value for the public, right?

There are always things people can complain about. Sorehead traditionalists always carp about the designated hitter rule. When the rule came in, we all said great, we can watch great all-round players like Al Kaline and Hank Aaron play longer. The tradition continues. Now youngsters learn to be designated hitters in their infancy, and we get to watch megastars like Ron Kittle, Cecil Fielder, and Carmen Castillo extend their careers. The soreheads point to the rules of baseball, particularly Rule Number One: "Baseball is a game between two teams of nine players." Big deal! Nine, ten, what's the difference?

The modern baseball fan looks forward to the day when the grand old game takes a tip from football and uses offensive and defensive teams — nine big galoots with Polish names to do the hitting, and a bunch of speedy Latin guys to catch everything. That'll be progress.

It's interesting that the designated hitter rule came into effect because the accounts figured out that Americans like to see lots of scoring. More people, they figured, would pay to see a 10-9 game than a 2-1 contest. The same reasoning killed soccer in North America. Who's going to watch a sport in which 1-1 is a real barnburner? Following this to its extreme, it seems peculiar that Americans have not clocked to cricket, a game in which a team that fails to score at least, oh, 300 runs in an inning is headed for obscurity. Americans also fail to turn up in great numbers to watch decathlons, a sport in which the winner is likely to rack up 8,000 points or so over two days.

And don't get me started on artificial turf. Honestly, some of these purists would have the boys out there in baggy flannel uniforms again. Artificial turf is fast, it's bouncy, it's a pretty pastel, it's high tech, it's America at its best. It has brought into modern baseball the most exciting play to be seen today — the ground rule double to straightaway centrefield. Look — how many times have you seen it happen? Your team's in trouble. The other guys have got a speedy Latin dude on first, and the hitter booms one over your centrefielder's head. Okay, José or Jésus or whatever his damn name is is already back in the dugout scarcely breathing hard, and the batter's thinking triple, maybe inside-the-park homer, when booooiiiiingggg! The balls hits the artificial turf and bounces clear over the fence. Ground rule double! Everybody goes back, and you still haven't given up a run. Then your manager pulls the pitcher four times and argues with the ump until it finally starts to rain or curfew is called or people just get bored and go home. It's the modern game.

Then there's basketball. These guys are so tall now, they've actually started a professional league for normal people. Why don't they just bring in a rule for the NBA that the five players on court at any given time can measure no more than 380 inches altogether? So if you've got a seven-footer out there, you've got to have somebody 5'8" or two guys 5'10" or some such arrangement. If nothing else, it would sure make the coaches think. Not only that, it would provide lucrative employment for people of a normal height who would like to use cocaine too.

Now, about football. Football's gotten completely out of hand. Football used to be a bad-weather game. We all grew up, those of any respectable age at all, huddled against the weather, watching guys in muddy brown uniforms bashing heads in the rain and muck. A couple of weeks later, they'd be sliding around in the snow. You had to respect these guys. They were athletes. And they were tough. And they played for peanuts too. No one said they were bright, but they sure were tough.

What have you got these days? A handful of guys who should be track stars or baseball players, and a whole lot of guys who should be sumo wrestlers. It's stupid, is what it is. The first thing you do is take a leaf out of baseball's book, and scrap these offensive and defensive teams. Everybody plays both ways. The fat guys couldn't lug that weight around for 60 minutes, and the frail guys couldn't take the pace. Bring back football players! Think of the payroll savings, for a start.

Okay, the next thing you do is play the game outdoors on grass. Artificial turf is brutal on football players, and it eliminates mud. Domes keep the rain and snow out, and take all the fun out of the game. Personally, I'd be just as happy to ban football altogether in places like Florida and California. Places like that are fine for baseball and golf and other warm-weather pursuits. Great places to retire. Lousy for real men, which is what football players used to be before they started wearing plastic shirts.

And where have all the challengers gone? Where did the USFL, the WFL, and the old Continental Football League go wrong? They copied all the same old tired rules and tried to compete with the NFL on its own turf. Big mistake. Let's use our imagination. Let's get the steroids and the squareheads out of football and make it a game we can be proud of once again!

EMILY PILLAR'S ETIQUETTE FOR THE EIGHTIES

Emily Pillar is acknowleged as the world's foremost authority on matters of correctness in social intercourse: "Etiquette is for us all, from the hoity-toity to the *hoi polloi*. Just because you wear a bowling shirt doesn't mean you have to act like a pig."

PIZZA ETIQUETTE

- The host shall place the telephone order. A useful guide for ordering is 3 slices per gentleman, 2 per lady.

- The wishes of anyone requesting anchovies may be ignored.

- It is acceptable to withold any gratuity to the delivery person if the pizza is cold, stuck to the lid, or shows evidence of having been partially eaten.

- Jalepeno and/or garlic pizzas should be consumed only by close friends in large, well-ventilated rooms.

- Loose slices of pepperoni shall be ceded to the slice on the right.

SEX

- Always remember your partners name.

PARTY ETIQUETTE

- BYOB means Bring Your Own Bottle. Rubbing liniments and cleaning products are not acceptable.

- RSVP means a response in writing is requested. FAX machine, laser printer or personal computer communications are unacceptable.

- Tootsie rolls are technically not *hors d'oeuvres*.

- When spiking the punch, more than three 'Jonestown' quips are excessive.

- It is acceptable practice for the hosts to serve less superior wines later in the evening. After 3 a.m., aftershave products may be substituted.

- "Popping one's cookies," "Driving the porcelain bus," or "Talking to Ralph on the big white phone," are all acceptable euphemisms for vomiting.

- It is impolite for hosts to feign death in order to hasten the departure of tarrying guests.

COHABITATION ETIQUETTE

- The gentleman shall cancel his subscriptions to *Penthouse*, *Velvet* and *Swank* magazines.

- The lady shall give away or store indefinitely all Don Johnson posters.

- Gentleman's novelty underwear (Home of the Whopper, etc.) shall only be worn by mutual consent.

- Both parties should ensure that toenails are well-trimmed.

- The television channel selector shall be shared equally, except in instances of professional football telecasts.

- The gentleman shall ensure he *always* puts the toilet seat back down in the middle of the night.

WHY WORK
FOR A LIVING
Or — How the Other Half Lives

1. Australian marathon runner Rob de Castella was invited to take part in the 1987 Los Angeles Marathon. His agent replied that Mr. de Castella was undertaking no races at the moment, but that for $50,000 he would state publicly that if he had been about to race, he would have done it in Los Angeles.

2. Pitcher Bill Caudill was paid $1,200,000 by the Toronto Blue Jays in 1987. To play for the Oakland Athletics!

3. Gerald Ford received $153,268 in 1986 to be neither president of the United States nor a U.S. representative. He also received $286,000 in federal funds for his office support. In addition he made more than $540,000 from companies for which he acts as a consultant or board member. He also earns approximately $400,000 per year from making speeches. The U.S. government spends more than $3,000,000 per year to protect him. This is *Gerald Ford* we're talking about.

4. Jessica Hahn received $115,000 from the PTL Club for having sex once with Rev. Jim Bakker. No one's saying it was pleasant, but

it's certainly a living wage. Actually Ms. Hahn was meant to get more than twice that amount, but once the story broke, the PTL Club welched on the remainder. The sum was conditional on Ms. Hahn's remaining silent about the tryst — as if anyone would boast about it! Jim and Tammy Faye were paid $1.6 million in 1986.

5. A typing error by Fawn Hall accidentally put $8,000,000 into the Swiss bank account of the Sultan of Brunei.

6. Between them, Fawn Hall, Vanna White, Donna Rice, and Jessica Hahn have been offered an estimated million dollars to pose nude for men's magazines.

7. Jerry Falwell announced that if 1,000 people gave him $1,000 each, he would plummet down a water slide fully clothed.

8. Wayne Newton — the Gerald Ford of showbiz — has made millions of dollars as an entertainer.

9. Peter Holm, some kind of Swedish pop musician nobody's ever heard of, was married to Joan Collins for thirteen months, and spent 1.3 million dollars. Then he took her to court for 1.2 million more, as well as $80,000 a month.

10. Then again, Joan Collins gets an estimated $95,000 a week to appear in "Dynasty," a television show that probably makes the Swedish pop scene sound like Vienna in the late eighteenth century.

BEST QUOTES FROM FAMOUS CYNICS

"The only way to be a success in Hollywood is to be as obnoxious as the next guy." *Peter Holm.*

"What's the difference?" *Yoko Ono*

"Freedom of the press is freedom to print such of the proprietor's prejudices as the advertisers don't object to." *Hannen Swaffer*

"Justice is open to all, like the Ritz Hotel." *Justice James Mathew*

"Give me chastity and continency — but not yet." *St. Augustine*

"The real reason we use language is not to more clearly express our desires, but to better conceal them. That is why we have euphemisms." *Oliver Goldsmith*

"It is not enough to succeed. Others must fail." *Gore Vidal*

"Whenever I hear the word culture, I release the safety-catch on my pistol." *Hanns Johst*

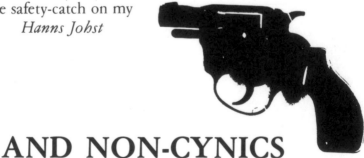

AND NON-CYNICS

"Sometimes when you have everything it's difficult to understand what really counts." *Christina Onassis*

"I go the way that Providence dictates with the assurance of a sleep-walker." *Adolf Hitler*

Cynics (circa 1987)